Citizens: Towards a Citizenship Culture

Citizens: Towards a Citizenship Culture

Edited by

Bernard Crick

Blackwell Publishers

Copyright © The Political Quarterly Publishing Co. Ltd.

ISBN 0–631–22856–X

First published 2001

Blackwell Publishers
108 Cowley Road, Oxford, OX4 1JF, UK

and

350 Main Street,
Malden, MA 02148, USA

British Library Cataloguing in Publication Data
A catalogue record for this book is available from the British Library

Library of Congress Cataloging in Publication Data
Citizens: towards a citizenship culture/edited by Bernard Crick.
    p. cm.
Includes bibliographical references and index.
ISBN 0–631–22856–X
1. Political culture—Great Britain. 2. Great Britain—Social conditions—1945– I. Title: At head of title: Political quarterly series. II. Crick, Bernard R.
JN231.C53 2001
306.2′0941–dc21   2001035494

Typeset by Joshua Associates Ltd, Oxford
Printed in the UK by Cambrian Printers, Aberystwyth

CONTENTS

Notes on Contributors

Yasmin Alibhai-Brown is a weekly columnist for *The Independent*, a writer and broadcaster. She is a senior research fellow at the Foreign Policy Centre, and author of *True Colours, Who Do We Think We Are?*, and *After Multiculturalism*.

Neal Ascherson was born in Edinburgh and has spent most of his life as a journalist. He has been a foreign correspondent specialising in central and eastern Europe, and in Scottish politics. His most recent book was *Black Sea* (1996). He contested Renfrewshire West for the Scottish Liberal Democrats at the first Scottish Parliament elections in 1999. He was the first winner of the Orwell Prize for political writing.

Anthony Barker is Reader in Government, University of Essex. Research interests include Whitehall and House of Commons reform and 'modernisation', notably their links with the major public inquiries and other policy review processes in the UK. Author of *Rule by Task Force*, 1999.

Michael Brunson is a freelance writer and broadcaster. He was Political Editor of ITN from 1968–2000, and, before that, was ITN's Washington Correspondent and Diplomatic Editor. At Westminster, he served as Chairman of both the Parliamentary Lobby Journalists and the Parliamentary Press Gallery. During 1998, he was a member of the Government's Advisory Group on Citizenship Education.

Colin Crouch is the current chairman and a former editor of *The Political Quarterly*, and author of the recent Fabian Society pamphlet *Coping with Post-Democracy*. He is a professor and chairman of the department of Social and Political Sciences at the European University Institute, Florence, and external scientific member of the Max Planck Institute for Social Research, Cologne.

Karen Evans holds the Chair in Education (Lifelong Learning) at the University of London, Institute of Education. She was previously Professor of Post-Compulsory Education at the University of Surrey. She has directed 15 major studies of learning and life transitions in Britain, Canada, and the wider European Union. Her book, *Learning and Work in the Risk Society* was published in 2000.

Anthony Everitt is a writer and a commentator on cultural policy. He is Visiting Professor in Visual and Performing Arts at Nottingham University. He was Secretary-General of the Arts Council of Great Britain. His life of Cicero was recently published by John Murray.

Isobel Lindsay is a Lecturer in the Department of Government at the University of Strathclyde. She held office in the Campaign for Scottish Parliament and in the Scottish Civic Forum, about which she has written widely.

Martin Linton is Labour MP for Battersea, a member of the Home Affairs Committee and a former journalist on the *Guardian*. He is a member of the Labour Campaign for Electoral Reform, and joint author of 'Making Votes count'. He was a Guardian Research Fellow at Nuffield College, where he published a paper on press influence in the 1992 election, 'Was it the Sun Wot Won It?, and a report on the funding of political parties, 'Money and Votes' for the IPPR.

© The Political Quarterly Publishing Co. Ltd. 2001
Published by Blackwell Publishers, 108 Cowley Road, Oxford OX4 1JF, UK and 350 Main Street, Malden, MA 02148, USA

John Maxton was MP for Glasgow, Cathcart from 1979 to 2001, before that a university lecturer in social studies and active in the adult education movement.

Joyce McMillan is chief theatre critic of *The Scotsman*, and a political/social columnist for the paper. She was a member in 1998–9 of the government's Consultative Steering Group on procedures for the new Scottish Parliament, and is now a council member of the Scottish Civic Forum.

Charles Pattie is Professor of Geography at the University of Sheffield.

Richard Pring is Professor of Educational Studies at the University of Oxford. He is editor of *British Journal of Educational Studies*. His most recent book is *The Philosophy of Educational Research*, 1999.

Tom Schuller is Dean of the Faculty of Continuing Education and Professor of Lifelong Learning at Birkbeck College, London. He is co-director of a new DFEE-funded research centre on the wider benefits of learning, and is a governor of the Working Men's College.

Patrick Seyd is Professor of Politics at the University of Sheffield.

Henry Tam is a social philosopher and public policy adviser. He is currently editing a collection of essays on progressive politics in the global age. His previous publications include: *Communitarianism: A New Agenda for Politics & Citizenship* (Macmillan); *Punishment, Excuses & Moral Development* (Avebury); *Marketing, Competition and the Public Sector* (Longman); *Serving the Public* (Longman); and *Responsibility and Personal Interactions* (Edwin Mellen Press). He has worked in both local and central government.

Matthew Taylor is Director of the Institute for Public Policy Research, Britain's leading centre left think tank. Until December 1998 he was Assistant General Secretary for the Labour Party. During the 1997 General Election he was Labour's Director of Policy and a member of the Party's central election strategy team.

Paul Whiteley is Professor of Government at the University of Essex.

Introduction

BERNARD CRICK

The aim of the ancients was the sharing of social power among the citizens of the same fatherland: this is what they called liberty. The aim of the moderns is the enjoyment of liberty in private pleasures; and they call liberty the guarantees accorded by institutions to these pleasures.

> [From Benjamin Constant, *The Liberty of the Ancients Compared with that of the Moderns*].

How can we become a citizen culture, a country whose inhabitants think it normal, right and even pleasurable to be concerned with and actively involved in public affairs? If ever sections of society were once going that way, we are now—for a multiplicity of reasons—drifting away fast. And by public affairs is not just meant the relationships of inhabitants to the state and government, but also to all those institutions intermediate and mediating between the individual and the state which we call civil society—on which in a free society the power and authority of government ultimately depends.

Each of the contributors to this book was asked to attempt an answer to this question in relation to an important sphere in which they were expert or greatly experienced. They were asked not to be concerned with the short-term issues of what is politically feasible in this next term of a new government's term of office, but to help lift all our eyes by offering middle and long-term proposals for how to realise a vision of such a culture looking towards the middle years of this new century. So to try to define some practical vision or realisable ideal of a more democratic and genuinely inclusive society.

The editor shared a thought with all the contributors without wishing to commit them to a reply: if the old 'forward march' of Labour as a democratic socialist project now seems either halted, indeed, or even abandoned, or at least no longer realisable in its former terms, that then in Britain we can at least, some say at best, aim to achieve a radically more democratic, inclusive and outward-looking society; and that this should reach all the way down from top to bottom, from the practices of central government and the parties to devolved national, regional and local institutions and practices. I suspect that the strange search for a 'Third Way' (either by people too busy to think or too prudent to commit themselves to anything specific)[1] was itself a title decided for a play before a script had been written, that this will settle down into what was perhaps implicit from the beginning: New Labour taking on the old mantle of radical democracy, stealing the Liberals' clothes (and they are good clothes—up to a point, that point being the pinch of poverty), even if not wishing openly to share a common cloak or mantle (which, of course, would imply electoral reform—which is why we lead with that).

Published by Blackwell Publishers, 108 Cowley Road, Oxford OX4 1JF, UK and 350 Main Street, Malden, MA 02148, USA

Bernard Crick

Not To Beg The Question

However, do we beg the question? Is the case really so overwhelming that this is a worthy cause, a social transformation—for such it would be—devoutly to be wished? Others would say that the greatest happiness of the greatest number is to be gained simply through the uninhibited working of the market, now indeed the global market, and that active citizenship or radical democracy would be too interventionist towards the economy, both on the state and the local level. Also one contributor to this book has serious doubts that the public accountability of government would be helped by a citizen culture, indeed I think he thinks it would be hindered; that a clear line of legal accountability and ministerial responsibility could get blurred by populist pressure. These are powerful arguments. And, of course, no sensible person should press the contrary arguments to extremes. Purely market values, total privatisation, would indeed destroy much of what is most valuable in the sociability of human life: that ultimately individual human identity is a relationship with others, mutual recognition and respect. But unqualified democracy can go too far. Beatrice Webb once remarked that 'democracy is not the multiplication of ignorant opinions'. Nor is the person who with passionate intensity gives their whole life to public affairs necessarily to be admired or trusted more than any other in the exercise of office.

So do we beg the question? Yes, we do; or at least we do not here aim to repeat yet again the arguments that there is a democratic deficit in British society and that market pricing need not involve market values. Three books in this same series have argued all this already.[2] We want to build on that and all the large bodies of writing, part the academic on 'civic republicanism' or on 'social capital' and part that of the finest columnists of the broadsheets, which have both been concerned with the broad and basic arguments of principle, but now to try to show in specific instances the case for a citizenship culture and then, perhaps less successfully, how it might operate. The latter is difficult to envisage for the clear reason that the free actions of free men and women are difficult to predict. Elsewhere I have mused[3] that it is curious, if commendable and perhaps hopeful, that governments of any hue, obsessed as they are with control and occupationally concerned with citizenship mainly as voting in public elections (and even that is qualified by private musings as to whether high turnout is helpful or not to the party), nonetheless support citizenship being taught in schools ('active' as well as 'good'); and they promote in many a speech 'volunteering' (perhaps secure in the knowledge that most volunteers will be told what to do, that most of our great national voluntary bodies are somewhat negative models of democratic participation). And different Ministries sponsor different episodes of local community development, usually as 'pilot projects' (few of which ever fly) rather than as consistent national policy. Nonetheless, all of this may be, I hope, stimulating trouble for the future.

There is another sense in which the question can be begged, as already hinted. Many of us point to the dangers of a society more and more dominated by consumerism linked to an aggressive revival of the Victorian work ethic. You work harder but you spend harder—thrift and savings have got lost somewhere along the road of unpremeditated social change. Family life as well as concern for public affairs suffer when, as survey results confirm observation, hours of work have increased and shopping and sport are people's main preferred activities in reduced leisure time. However, to affirm the primacy in the good life of concern for others and for public values is not to say, as some of us thinking in the Aristotelian and civic-republican tradition of European political thought have come near to saying, that the good man and woman *must be* an active citizen. A moral philosopher, Mark Philp, has written in a recent essay, 'Citizenship and Integrity', that it is not difficult to see the appeal of citizenship in the civic republican or classical mode, and why people should (like ourselves) seek to restore it: 'The vision of a virtuous, active citizenry, engaged in deliberation on the proper ends of their association and taking turns at ruling and being ruled—especially when coupled with the assumption that civic virtue provides the natural completion of the broader moral virtues.' But he points out that this positive view of *citizen* has little moral significance for most people, almost wholly immersed in private concerns, however selfish or predatory. 'It is entirely possible to believe that [some of] those who live private lives may live more virtuously.' His first point is what we now seek to change, but to do so must involve accepting his second point. Perhaps the civic ideal had best be stated as the will to lead both a rich public and a rich private life, and the opportunities and skills to move easily from the one to the other. Indeed having made his humanistic or 'sceptical caveats', he does assert that 'modern democratic states will be politically stable only if most of their citizens see compliance with their civic responsibilities as a requirement of personal integrity.'[4]

What Is To Be Done?

Do or you are done by. The obstacles to effective doing are, however, great. Much of the nearly free daily entertainment of the popular media seems a form of bread and circuses, either consciously or unconsciously designed to divert people from real issues. There is something in the theories of the old Marxists of the Frankfurt School that capitalism controls not by force but by cultural degradation. Orwell somehow picked this up in his grim satire *Nineteen Eighty-Four:* the Ministry of Truth itself produced prolefeed for the masses including 'rubbishy newspapers containing almost nothing except sport, crime and astrology, sensational five cent novelettes, films oozing with sex, and sentimental songs which were composed entirely by mechanical means on a special kind of kaleidoscope known as a versificator.' But our present press is not uniquely to blame. The tactic of *panem et circenses*, bread and circuses, is as old as fears of the potential power of the people:

From sunrise until evening, in sunshine and in rain, they stand open-mouthed examining minutely the good points and the bad points of the charioteers and their horses. And it is most remarkable to see an innumerable crowd of plebeians, their minds filled with a kind of eagerness, hanging on the outcomes of the chariot race. These and similar things prevent anything memorable or serious being done in Rome.
[a 4th century A.D. writer in Res Gestae XIV, 7, 25f.]

Today it is tax cuts, Domes and spinning wheels. But perhaps the noble Roman missed the point. To prevent anything serious may have been the point.

What is to be done? The contributors will speak for themselves. But before I underline or gloss a few points: let me name and briefly explain some key dimensions that we have ignored, mainly because we all take them for granted or because they are part of the problem that we believe a citizen culture could, if not wholly cure, at least abate. Even the Countess of Wessex is aware that prime ministers are increasingly adopting a presidential style; and were she even brighter she might have pointed to a growing American-isation of campaigning techniques and media manipulation among the inner circle of the younger political advisers. Quite specifically many of them had a common experience in following, even participating in, Clinton's first presidential campaign. They then longed to do that here. The machinery of government is now used more for central control or for popular show than for functional efficiency, certainly not to ensure responsiveness to informed opinion. The Treasury and the Home Office are in the first category and the weird range of functions under the magic word 'Environment' is meant to impress, just as Department for Education *and* Employment was meant to imply that there will be jobs for all if everyone has the right training, and so the emphasis shifts to training rather than (so they say) outmoded ideas of education.[5] Perhaps the two biggest problems are the appallingly low standard of political debate set by the leaders of the main parties—sound-bite recrimination rather than reasoned exposition of principles and policy;[6] and, not unconnected, the growing alienation of young people from public and political commitments. The first could begin to change if a prime minister or a leader of the opposition by personal example willed it to change, despite the popular press; even by challenging the popular press. Many of us had a hope of this that has been dashed. The second will only change if public expectations rise to demand a lasting uplift of debate and far greater provision for and trust in participation. That is our concern in this book.

The questions of electoral and parliamentary reform are plainly linked. John Maxton's parthian shot as an MP sets out strongly what MPs could do for themselves to make parliament a more effective check on the executive and to restore its credibility as the voice of the nation, now so much by-passed both by No 10 and the media. What price 'modernisation' when it comes to parliament? But is the power of the whips ever likely to be broken unless electoral reform, meaning proportional representation, not just the window-dressing of the Alternative Vote, gives individual MPs greater security in

4

selection in their own constituencies and makes the business of carrying votes in the Commons as uncertain as it is and will be in any acceptable reformed second chamber? Nonetheless, Martin Linton's acceptance of the 'Jenkins system' as a realistic *first step* has much to commend it, especially if coupled, as he proposes, with a two-question referendum, as was done in the Scottish referendum. Once 'first past the post' is modified, however inadequately, the greater matter will never rest. That is precisely why many of 'the turkeys who fear Christmas' are against any move whatever (except where political necessity forces, as in Northern Ireland, Wales and Scotland already). The political difficulties are great, as if 'the body politic performing open heart surgery on itself. It is awkward. It is painful. But I think it will be done.' If it is not done, it will be next to impossible for New Labour to move (as I suspect its leaders wish) from an ideology or public philosophy of muted social democracy to a strident radical democracy; or move they may try, but they will not be taken seriously.

Several pressure groups within the Labour Party itself see reforms to party democracy as the key to democratic reform in general. They are by no means all 'Old Labour': some have the Charter 88 new liberal faith that constitutional reform by itself can set all to rights—economic questions are either secondary or will inevitable follow. Mathew Taylor challenges such thinking. He sees the problem of 'civic disengagement' as arising from the very control that parties themselves exercise over the democratic process. While party leaders may go on about parties getting closer to communities, this 'belies their desire to maximize discipline.' For 'the voice of local communities will tend to be loudest when opposing public authorities.' He points out that community activists 'are increasingly unlikely to see political parties as the most fruitful channel for the pursuit of their interests.'[7] The better role of local parties is 'not to act as a closed shop' (as if they know what people want simply by virtue of being elected—because they wanted to be elected, gave endless evenings to it and were elected, moreover by very small numbers), but 'to offer support to those in the community who share its broad values.' I think local parties have to face these truths unpleasant to them, just as MPs must come to see that the despite into which they have fallen has much to do with their grim addiction to party loyalty on all major issues.

Scottish devolution admittedly arose—and in the strong form that it did—because otherwise, as the late Donald Dewar pummelled into the heads of his Cabinet colleagues, ignoring all fancy arguments , the SNP might have come to dominate Scotland. But being there, for whatever reason, the United Kingdom constitution and its politics can never be the same again, as Joyce McMillan argues. In fact it works pretty well, despite many believing the contrary thanks to the London media (either from ignorance, laziness or economy) taking most of their views on Scotland from the strongly anti-devolution *Scotsman*, doing everything it can to discredit the parliament, rather than from more balanced and open pages of the *Herald*. But here is the spectacle of PR and a coalition government working in a parliament whose procedures have been, like those of the Welsh Assembly, a radical break from Westminster—more democratic, more open and more efficient in its use of time. If regional government comes at least to parts of England, it is likely that rules of procedure will draw a great deal on the Scottish and Welsh experience—unless they are centrally imposed from the start as last-ditch attempts to appear devolutionist and democratic while seeking to retain a centralist uniformity.

If one accepts that now the United Kingdom has to be conceived and managed as a multi-national state, the problems raised by how best to deal with racism and to what degree the idea of multiculturalism should be mirrored in legislation and education become manageable. Yasmin Alibhai-Brown sees 'the vocabulary of citizenship' as a linking factor. She is plainly aware of the dangers of the language of 'group rights' as if groups can have the same rights as individuals, which would, for one thing, imply that groups should have rights against their own members who may wish to leave, perhaps to marry out or to prevent others marrying in. Some of the advocacy of 'multiculturalism' as a new over-riding reconstruction of Britishness has been more demanding than thoughtful. We can, indeed, and should celebrate diversity but within the context of a citizen culture. She quotes admirable words of Gordon Brown: 'As the Tebbit "cricket test" and the Stephen Lawrence case illustrate, there are those who would retreat from an expansive idea of Britishness into a constricted shell of right wing nationalism. My vision of Britain comes not from uniformity but from celebrating diversity, in other words a multi-ethnic and a multinational Britain—outward looking, open, internationalist with a commitment to democracy and tolerance.' May one respectfully ask a Chancellor of the Exchequer to be sure to put some money where his mouth is? Celebrations and democratic institutions (if that means devolution) do not always come cheap. Neal Ascherson similarly links a recognition of diversity in our own midst to a citizen culture that can rise above a narrow nationalism to see that what we share with Europe is a respect for free institutions. And one must not rub salt into Europhobic wounds by noting that the idea of a positive, political citizenship is stronger in most of the EC states than in a Britain still bound by traditions of the law-abiding subject of the Crown. I begin to see why nearly all of those who opposed citizenship education in schools were against the Economic Community in principle. Traditionally we have not needed these kind of things and therefore we do not need them now.

Education, Media and Community

Anthony Everitt writing on the liveliness of the multiplicity of local Arts groups as themselves examples of people acting together as citizens, says that the problem is 'how to support without smothering'—a problem of which both Isobel Lindsay, writing on the voluntary sector, and Henry Tam extolling community action as the very root of citizenship are both fully aware.

There is a real danger that voluntary bodies and charities, sometime even more informal community groups, can end up tied by grants as virtual agents of the state. And not all the democratic credentials of these bodies are impeccable. However, they are main vehicles for any realistic hopes to create a citizen culture. Funding my membership subscription is inadequate in deprived areas, where need is greatest, and even in mixed areas usually reduces organisers to fundraisers. Appeals are at the mercy of fashion and giving, while good in itself, seldom responds to rational criteria of need. Ways of central funding must be found that are under local control other than, vide Matthew Taylor's argument, by party caucus in town hall. Core funding for Civic Forums on the Scottish model could be the answer who might then break down the pounds into useful pennyweights precisely targeted to local needs. Lots of little sums are needed for which central control is always too cumbersome. As with some Foundations, central government too often finds it cost-inefficient to dispense small grants.

Accountability need not, like school inspection, be annual unless there are real problems; and accountability certainly should not demand uniformity of practice. The press attack central bureaucracy in one breath and then raise alarms in relation to medical procedures about 'the lottery of where you live'. But the answer to that is to lead a more intense civic life where you live. (As again both Henry Tam and Isobel Lindsay argue so cogently.) Politicians should defend diversity of practice. Devolution cannot mean uniformity. Local democracy does not mean that all public services should be the same everywhere. A few hard cases will inevitably occur. The press can have it both ways, all too easily: 'government interference!' and 'scandalous anomaly!' Michael Brunson sees the faults of the media but also the dangers of thinking that there are radical solutions. There may not be solutions by routes of public controls, but that is no reason for governments not to answer back. He does not share my view of the popular press as the great dis-educator of our times. He sees signs of improvement, although he deplores 'life-style' rather than policy reporting and sees the need to give high quality explanations of the facts as well as the facts. But improvement is not a chicken and egg problem. He argues that if people want better newspapers, they will eventually get them. That leads us to education.

The 1998 report *Education for Citizenship and the Teaching of Democracy in Schools* ambitiously stated:

We aim at no less than a change in the political culture of this country both nationally and locally: for people to think of themselves as active citizens, willing, able and equipped to have an influence on public life and with the critical capacities to weigh evidence before speaking and acting; to build on and to extend radically to young people the best in existing traditions of community involvement and public service, and to make them individually confident in finding new forms of involvement and action among themselves.

Richard Pring endorses the subsequent decision for Citizenship to be added to the national curriculum, but rightly sees that on its own it is bound to fail in its full aspirations unless there are changes, over which admittedly it could itself have some influence, in the character of the whole curriculum—still too rigid and still either too vocational or too academically-orientated at too early an age. A genuine citizen culture will be based, as the whole western tradition of civic republicanism has been, on humanistic as well as technical values. The idea of a liberal education has taken a hard knock in the maintained sector but is essential for a free society not entirely either work or entertainment dominated. Tom Schuller and Karen Evans both argue the need for opportunities for education in general, for citizenship in particular, to continue life-long and to influence the world of work, not to be its instrument. Business itself is not entirely unaware that claims to be left alone and a lack of a dialogue about the other claims on the lives of employees and managers could soon prove counter-productive. If things were once over-regulated, now cultural images of work-to-consume coupled with devil-take-the-hindmost may have gone too far, and harsher political reactions can set in if ordinary people are not brought more into thought and participation.

We have been fortunate that the first results of the huge ESRC financed 'Citizen Audit', conducted by Patrick Seyd, Paul Whiteley and Charles Pattie could be reported in this volume. Overall the audit reveals relatively strong social capital: one in three of their respondents devote more than an hour a week in *some form* of voluntary activity. There is thus a base to build upon. But also one in three are dissatisfied with democracy.[8] They conclude that we are, indeed, 'right to be concerned about the levels of public disillusionment in the formal body politic.'

The answer must be found in stimulating democracy in the grass roots and local communities. The state would then have to adjust itself to these new and less manipulable pressures.

Notes

1 See for example Antony Giddens, *The Third Way: the renewal of social democracy*, Polity Press, 1998, a book of well-meaning abstract generalities curiously or cautiously avoiding any inferences to policy.
2 Colin Crouch and David Marquand, eds., *Reinventing Collective Action*, 1995; Paul Hirst and Sunil Khilnani, *Reinventing Democracy*, 1996; and Andrew Gamble and Tony Wright, *The New Social Democracy*, 1999, all published by Blackwell for *The Political Quarterly*.
3 Bernard Crick, *In Defence of Politics*, 5th ed, Continuum 2000; and *Essays on Citizenship*, Continuum 2000.
4 Mark Philp in Alan Montefiore and David Vines, eds., *Integrity in the Public and Private Domains*, London, Routledge 1998, pp. 20–21.
5 Apart from IT, medicine, engineering and law etc., how do we know in such a 'rapidly changing economic environment' etc. what we are training for? That's a difficult one, so the idea of 'key skills' has been invented that all in pre-18 education must follow (except that the academic streams pay little attention to these well-

meant abstractions—they are for the others). If you don't know what key skills are, the three 'hard' and the three 'soft', it would take too long to explain. I just mention it.

6 See my meditative polemic, 'The Decline of Political Thinking in British Public Life' in *Critical Review of International Social and Political Philosophy*, No. 1 Spring 1998; reprinted in *Essays on Citizenship*, op. cit.

7 The concept of 'community activist' still worries some. A recent government advisory committee wishing to advise that FE colleges should be specially funded to run training courses in citizenship for community activists was officially advised to call them 'community leaders' What's in a name? Quite a lot apparently.

8 See also Alison Park, 'Young People and Political Apathy' in Roger Jowell et al., *British Social Attitudes*, Vol. 16, Ashgate, 1999. And Colin Crouch, *Coping with Post-Democracy*, London, Fabian Society, 2001, offers a cogent and comprehensive analysis, much in tune with the themes of this book.

Options for the Referendum on the Voting System

MARTIN LINTON

WHEN I was elected to Parliament in 1997, I felt confident that we were going to see the greatest overhaul of the British constitution in fifty years. And in most respects we have. We have established a Scottish Parliament, a Welsh Assembly, a Bill of Rights and a Freedom of Information Act. We have started the reform of the House of Lords and we have introduced new voting systems in elections for Europe, for Scotland, for Wales and for London.

But a new voting system for the Commons? Well, all the radicalism seemed to evaporate as soon as we got to that. It was a disappointment to me, as I have always regarded the reform of our electoral system as the most crucial and most central part of our constitutional reform programme. But I suppose we always knew that it was also going to be the most problematical.

Ever since John Smith first proposed it, the pledge to hold a referendum on the voting system has led a precarious life. It has survived attempts to kill it off at Labour Party conferences in 1995 and 1998 and there was a trade-union-backed attempt to swamp the Labour Party's internal consultation on the referendum. Finally, at the Labour Party's National Policy Forum in Exeter there was a union-backed attempt to keep it out of the election manifesto, but it failed to gain enough support and the referendum remains in place as one of Labour's key constitutional commitments.

It was not just the trade unions. The most reluctant supporters of the Government on this issue are to be found among my colleagues in the Commons. I helped to organise a series of regional briefings for MPs by members of the Independent Commission on the Voting System—the Jenkins Commission—and their academic experts and I have to say there was precious little enthusiasm for the report. On paper there are well over 100 Labour MPs who support electoral reform, but not many of them are keen to stand up and be counted when the mood of the Parliamentary Labour Party appears to be so strongly 'anti-Jenkins'. At the briefings we got about 30 Labour MPs in all, out of 418, but what was depressing was not so much the numbers as the questions. The first question was always about the boundary reviews that would be necessary if the Jenkins system were to be adopted.

The Last Converts

Maybe MPs were always going to be the last converts. They, after all, are elected by the system and some of them find it difficult to believe that there can be anything wrong with a system that elected them. I have been castigated by colleagues for suggesting that MPs might somehow be motivated by self-interest when they spring to the defence of first-past-the-post. I'll concede that self-interest may not be the right word. But there is a kind of optical illusion that can easily make MPs blind to the faults of the system. They point out that when they go back to their constituencies 'no one ever talks about voting systems in the pub' or 'no one ever comes to lobby me about electoral reform in my surgeries'. It doesn't seem to occur to them that they are probably talking to people who voted for them and are going to be happy with the voting system, almost by definition. They voted Labour and got a Labour MP. And if they voted for another party, they are hardly going to mention it. Nobody goes to their MP and says 'I didn't vote for you, but I'd like you to help me to take my case to the benefits tribunal'.

MPs do not speak to Labour supporters in other constituencies whose votes are regularly wasted, and they do not hear from non-Labour voters in their own seats who may be frustrated with the system. So I think this is one subject on which voters should not listen to MPs. In any case, it is not the place of elected representatives to decide how they should be elected. Systems of elections are the property of the voter. They must decide it directly in a referendum. Or as John Smith said, voting systems are too important to be left to MPs.

I take comfort from what happened in New Zealand. When they held their first non-binding plebiscite in September 1992 the great majority of MPs urged their supporters to tick the box that said 'I vote to retain the present first-past-the-post system'. In the event an overwhelming 85 per cent ticked the other box which said 'I vote for a change to the voting system'. It was generally acknowledged that it was the MPs' support for FPTP that contributed to its overwhelming defeat. In the subsequent binding referendum in November 1993 the MPs were advised to keep their heads down and the main parties resolved to take no collective stance, even though it was well known that the leadership of both parties supported retention of 'first-past-the-post'. In that referendum the result was much closer, but the forces of reform still defeated the entire political establishment by 54 to 46 per cent..

The one big difference in New Zealand was that they had a two-stage referendum. The second binding referendum was held on the same day as a general election and the new voting system, very similar to the Jenkins proposal, became law without further reference to Parliament. That gave the civil service three years to get the new voting system ready in time for the subsequent election.

The most time-consuming part of this job was the redrawing of constituency boundaries. In New Zealand they had to reduce them from 90 to 65. Under the 'minimum-change' version of the Jenkins proposal the number of constituencies in the UK would have to be reduced from 659 to 561. Roughly every sixth constituency would disappear and the adjoining constituencies would expand to absorb it. There already is a review due to be completed in the next

Parliament, but a change of system would mean the review would have to be far more fundamental. It would have to involve every constituency, whereas previous reviews have usually left a quarter or a third of the seats unchanged.

Once the new boundaries are drawn, there has to be time for the parties to decide which MP is going to fight which seat, a process which can be invidious in a normal boundary review but would be even more like a game of musical chairs when every sixth seat is disappearing, even though it will re-appear as a top-up seat.

To have a new system in place in time for the subsequent election would mean having the referendum in the first year of a new parliament. Ideally in the first six months. That seems most unlikely to happen. A referendum would first need an Act of Parliament to allow it to happen. And now, under the new Political Parties, Elections and Referendums Act which came into force in February 2001, there is a procedure to follow and a timetable for designating 'permitted participants' supporting for each possible outcome— the umbrella bodies that will conduct the campaigns.

In any case, a freshly re-elected Prime Minister may not want to rush into a Referendum Bill and then a referendum campaign so soon after an election. Indeed, it is clear he would prefer to have the referendum later in the Parliament after the Scottish and Welsh elections of 2003, but that raises all sorts of potential difficulties. First, if the new voting system cannot be used for the next election but only the election after that, then will the result be binding? The theory of the sovereignty of parliament implies that a parliament cannot bind its successor. Would the Government really be bound? And would the Opposition be bound if it were to win the subsequent election? Would it be open to the Opposition under Michael Portillo, or whoever is leader by then, to campaign in the subsequent election on the basis that they would set aside the result of the referendum?

If so, then a referendum held later than the first year of the next Parliament can only really offer the prospect of a new voting system on the assumption that Labour wins the subsequent election. To assume this means assuming that the Conservatives will suffer a third successive defeat, something I regard as devoutly to be desired, but I am conscious of the fact that it has never happened before.

It would also mean holding an election under a voting system that the electorate had already voted to change. That is no problem if the vote is decisive and would have elected the same party to government under either system, but a close result could lead to a constitutional nightmare. We have already seen how a narrow and contested result can undermine the legitimacy and authority of a president in the United States. It would be far worse if a party were elected narrowly under a voting system the electorate has already voted to scrap, especially if it is clear that it would have lost under the system the electorate has already voted for.

So is there an alternative? Fortunately, Tony Blair has two alternatives he can turn to. The first would be to call the referendum not on the Alternative

Vote Plus system recommended by the Jenkins Commission, but more straightforwardly on the Alternative Vote without the plus.

The argument against this course of action is clear: it would be a breach of the undertaking given in the 1997 election manifesto to hold a referendum in which voters would be offered 'a proportional alternative to the first-past-the-post system'. The Alternative Vote is not, in anyone's book, a system of proportional representation. It is true that—more often than not—it would be a little more proportional than first-past-the-post. If it had been used in the last two decades, it would have slightly reduced the Conservative majority in 1983 and 1992 (by about 20 seats), though it would have slightly increased the Conservative majority in 1987 and in 1997 it would have increased Labour's majority substantially from 179 to 245 and made the result even more disproportional.[1] It is true that 1997 was a very atypical election in that the second preferences of Liberal Democrat voters, usually balanced fairly evenly between the two main parties, were skewed very strongly in Labour's favour, so it would be perverse to judge AV on the basis of how it would have worked in 1997. Indeed one can argue that the Alternative Vote is in another sense much more proportional to voters' wishes, because it takes both their first and subsequent preferences into account. But by the standard definition of 'proportionality' it is not significantly more proportional that first-past-the-post.

Against this, there would be a number of arguments in favour of a referendum on the Alternative Vote. The first is that it would be a smaller and more understandable change from first-past-the-post. All MPs would be elected from constituencies, as at present, and the only visible change would be the instruction at the head of ballot paper. Instead of putting an 'x' against the candidate of their choice, voters would be asked to put the candidates in order of preference, with a '1' against their first choice, a '2' against their second and so on.

This could be seen as an organic change, an evolution from the present system rather than a seismic shift. It might be considered more in keeping with an approach to constitutional change which is gradual and incremental. Instead of offering the two changes recommended by the Jenkins Commission at the same time, it would take a 'one-step-at-a-time' approach, while leaving to the future the option of a referendum on the establishment of top-up seats.

The strongest argument in favour of this approach would, however, be the practical one. It could be implemented without the further complication of a boundary review at the next election. The only change required, apart from a public information campaign, would be in the wording of the ballot papers. The danger of constitutional gridlock would be averted.

Two Questions Not One

There is, however, another alternative open to Tony Blair that would avoid the charge that he was reneging on a commitment given at the last election.

He could hold a two-question referendum, asking voters first whether they want a preferential system (electing their constituency MP on a '1,2,3' system instead of a simple 'x' system as at present) and secondly whether they want a top-up system (electing one or two MPs for their county or district as well as a single MP for their constituency).

There would be nothing new about a two-question referendum. It was the solution the Government adopted in the referendum on Scottish devolution. On that occasion it wanted to ensure that the principle of a devolved parliament was not swamped by the issue of whether the parliament should have tax-raising powers. In the event both questions yielded a 'yes' answer, but by different majorities.

In this case a two-question approach would have additional advantages. It would simplify the issues in the public mind by unscrambling the two separate reforms rolled into one by the Jenkins Commission. These two reforms correspond to the two main problems thrown up by the present voting system—tactical voting and wasted votes. Tactical voting can be resolved by preferential voting, whereas wasted votes can only be addressed by the introduction of top-up seats.

The important point is that neither of these reforms depends on the other. While they have been offered as a package, they could be adopted as discrete solutions to discrete problems. Australia is an example of a country that has preferential voting without top-up seats. Closer to hand, Scotland and Wales have top-up seats without preferential voting. As a result tactical voting dilemmas persist in Scottish Parliament and Welsh Assembly elections and the problem of wasted votes still exists for some Australian voters. But the key point here is that the two-question approach passes the test: each possible set of answers ('yes/yes', 'yes/no', 'no/yes' and 'no/no') represents a rational preference and a realistic policy option.

Some may even feel that the two-question approach is in any case more palatable, as it avoids giving the voters the impression that they are being bounced into a bigger reform than they bargained for. It will treat voters with more respect, inviting them to form opinions on more complex issues and giving them more options to choose from. It will also be more challenging for politicians. A single question referendum would have put them in pro-Jenkins and anti-Jenkins camps where the issues might be more difficult to discern. But two questions will force all politicians to clarify exactly what they are for and against. It would be much easier for the Conservatives, for instance, to say they were against the 'Jenkins system' than to explain why they wanted to refuse the voter the right to indicate first and second preferences, as London voters have already done in their mayoral election in 2000.

But the crucial advantage of the two-question approach is again the practical one. In the event that there is a majority in favour on each question, the Government has two mandates, one to introduce a preferential voting system and the second to introduce top-up seats. Neither is dependent on the other and therefore each one can be introduced on its own time scale. Preferential voting can be introduced in the election that will be due in 2005–6 and top-up seats will have to wait until the Electoral Commission has had time to complete the boundary reviews which will be, at the earliest, three years after the referendum.

Other Existing Ways

The crucial question, of course, is whether a referendum will result in a majority for change of any kind. Opinion polls can't tell us very much. They show that the public supports reform of the voting system more often than not, but it all depends on the wording of the question and the timing. The public likes the idea of greater fairness in the voting system and it doesn't object to the idea of proportionality, but it doesn't care for post-election bartering or coalitions. Nor does it like the idea of 'weak government'. But the public's views are fairly fluid. Much will depend on the way the debate develops during the course of a referendum campaign.

The public's views about new voting systems are likely to be influenced by experience with proportional voting systems so far. Voters in Scotland, Wales and London have already voted in a two-vote election with constituency candidates on one side and a party list on the other. Voters in the whole country have had the chance to vote for a party list in the European Elections of 1999. A significant number of people objected to the system used in the European Elections, because they did not have the chance to vote for or against any individual candidate. But there was no similar objection to the system used in Scotland, Wales and London, which are closer to the system proposed in the Jenkins Report. Certainly, people did not find it difficult to follow the instructions on the ballot paper. There was no sudden increase in the number of spoilt ballots. Turnout in the Scotland Parliament election was 59 per cent—which was about what one would expect, halfway between what is normal in national and local elections. In Wales turnout in the Assembly elections was more disappointing at 46 per cent, struggling to equal the traditionally high local election turnout in Wales. Turnout in the 1999 European elections was only 23 per cent, down 13 points since the last Euro-elections in 1995. However, that was mirrored by a similar drop in the local elections turnout a month earlier—from 41 to 29 per cent—and the turnout in a parliamentary by-election on the same day was even lower at 19.5 per cent. Absence of protest votes, election fatigue, apathy, cynicism—all of these may have played a part—but there is no evidence linking the drop in turnout with the change in voting system.

The more reasonable assumption is that these new voting systems, once established, will have the effect of increasing voter turnout. No one would argue that a voting system will ever be a major factor in determining the level of participation in elections when there are so many other potential factors. But a reluctant voter, half an hour from close of poll, with the rain pouring down, will always ask himself the same three questions: Will the outcome of the election make a difference to me? Is it going to be a close election? And could my vote make a difference?

The voting system can only have a bearing on the last on these three questions. The very high level of wasted votes in the first-past-the-post system means that a high proportion of voters believe that their votes cannot make a difference. Not only is there a high proportion of votes that turn out, with hindsight, to have been wasted, but in first-past-the-post there is a high proportion of voters who know in advance that their vote is bound to be wasted, either because their candidate cannot win or, indeed, because their candidate is bound to win.

This is a feature that is unique to first-past-the-post and is, in my view, the main reason for the significantly lower turnout in first-past-the-post countries. According to the International Institute for Democracy and Electoral Assistance[2] the average turnout in first-past-the-post countries is 58 per cent compared with 66 per cent in countries that use the alternative vote and 67 per cent in countries that use mixed systems, like the Alternative Vote Plus, or List systems of proportional representation.

In the international league table of election turnout during the 1990s the United Kingdom is ranked 65th and the United States, using the same system, 138th. Turnout levels can be correlated to many other factors, including levels of literacy, though not wealth, human development and the competitiveness of election contests, but none of these would help to explain why countries like the UK and the US should be so low.

In the latter case it is undoubtedly helped by archaic voter registration laws that still put the onus on individuals to register as voters rather than on the state to ensure that everyone is registered. But the voting system is the factor which can do most to explain the poor performance of the UK as a participative democracy in comparison with the rest of Western Europe. 'Participation rates in British elections are either the lowest or the equal lowest among the larger Western European democracies In the 1997 general election turnout was 71 per cent. In the 1998 local elections average turnout was 40 per cent. In the last European elections turnout was 23 per cent.'[3]

First-past-the-post is a widespread system used by no less than 68 countries around the world and covering 45 per cent of the world's population. But the names of countries that use it hardly inspire confidence. 'Afghanistan, Antigua, Aruba, Bahamas, Barbados, Belize, Bhutan, Botswana, Burma. . . .' and ending with 'Virgin Islands, Yemen, Zaire, Zambia and Zimbabwe.' It soon becomes apparent that all the countries are either former British colonies or countries in the early stages of democratisation.

A number of former British colonies have already been through the process of switching away from first-past-the-post, including Australia and New Zealand. More recently, South Africa adopted the List PR system for its first universal suffrage election. What is equally significant is that none of the new democracies in Eastern Europe has adopted first-past-the-post.

16

The last country to do so was Papua-New Guinea and there it has been a disaster.

We are aware of the fact that first-past-the-post can elect MPs on low shares of the poll, famously with only 26 per cent of the vote in Inverness, Nairn and Lochaber in 1992. But in Papua-New Guinea every village put up a candidate and almost half the MPs have less than 20 per cent of the vote. One MP was elected on 6.3 per cent. The country has had a series of weak, multi-party coalition governments, often changing in between elections. Other countries have experienced the opposite problem of first-past-the-post—it can very easily create one-party states. In Mauritius one party took all the seats on just 65 per cent of the vote and the opposition was left unrepresented.[4]

First-past-the-post must be one of the most unhappy legacies of the British empire, but once you have a voting system and all your MPs are elected by that system it is very difficult to manage the process of change. It is easier with some major external impetus, such as independence or defeat in war, but to change system in other circumstances requires politicians to take a few steps back and look at the electoral system in a cold dispassionate light.

The 'Jenkins system' does not offer a panacea that will cure all of these ills. But it is a system that has been remarkably well crafted to suit the particular circumstances and concerns of the British voting public. Given an open debate and a fair wind, I certainly do not despair of the chances of persuading the public to support it. But I do not underestimate the problems either. This is not like reforming an outside institution, even the House of Lords, which can be done with detachment, even with gusto. This is more like the body politic performing open heart surgery on itself. It is awkward. It is painful. But I think it will be done.

Notes

1 *The Alternative Vote and the UK General Elections 1983–1997*, London, Charter 88, 2000.
2 Voter Turnout from 1945 to 1997: a Global Report.
3 Home Affairs Committee 4th Report on Electoral Law and Administration.
4 The International IDEA Handbook of Electoral System Design.

Party Democracy and Civic Renewal

MATTHEW TAYLOR

In this chapter I set out to examine aspects of the relationship between party democracy, civic renewal and popular participation in collective decision-making. I would reject the idea that reforms to party democracy are either the cause or a significant solution to the problem of civic disengagement. Instead I suggest that it is the very control exercised by parties over the democratic process that has come to be a major impediment to democratic renewal. The chapter recommends action to break up the party cartel in our nation's political life and—with a particular focus on local government—makes some tentative suggestions for how this might begin.

'Party', 'Democracy', 'Civic Engagement'

Juxtaposing the concepts 'party' and 'democracy' in the context of a discussion of civic engagement can lead to two very different types of analysis. The first sees changes—nearly always portrayed in negative terms—in the nature of party democracy as having a detrimental effect on civic engagement. So, for example, Pete Smith writing in the journal *Representation:* 'Turning the party into a voiceless agent of the powerful, an unspeakable tool of the charmed circle, is the next step in hollowing out the democratic process. The elite, the privileged, the well connected are able to dominate the decision making process regardless of which party is in power. Political parties once gave ordinary people a say in the political process. Whilst claiming to modernise them the intention is clear—abolish them.'[1]

The second analysis stands back from a discussion of the workings of internal democracy of parties tending to see this dynamic as more complex, more externally determined or less independently significant than commentators like Smith. Instead the focus is the effect of parties on the health of democracy and the level of civic engagement. As Tom Ellis writes: '. . . a democracy cannot allow party to be a private institution, even if functioning on lines acceptable to Pete Smith. Party must be accountable to the public not just its members. Nor is the opportunity to reject a party once every five years a sufficient measure of accountability.'[2]

This chapter favours the second of these approaches, breaking up the party cartel that is clogging the arteries of political participation. Before elaborating on this, the argument that a renewal of party democracy is the path to a renewal of civic engagement in politics must be addressed.

© The Political Quarterly Publishing Co. Ltd. 2001
Published by Blackwell Publishers, 108 Cowley Road, Oxford OX4 1JF, UK and 350 Main Street, Malden, MA 02148, USA

1979–2001 Labour and Myth of Party Democracy

Focusing on Britain and the recent history of the Labour Party in particular shows party democracy to be an elusive and contingent phenomenon. Three decades ago, in response to the perceived failure of the 1974–79 government and in particular the rejection of the draft manifesto prepared by Party activists and officers in preference to that of the leadership, the left of the Labour Party developed a set of demands to 'democratise' it . But the image of democracy promoted by groups such as the Campaign for Labour Party Democracy was one that sought to put control not in the hands of ordinary members but instead in those of union officials and Party activists. The result of the partial success of this movement was undoubtedly seen in an increase in internal debate in the Labour Party at all levels. However, far from strengthening the Party and its contribution to civic activism this debate contributed to opening a yawning chasm between the concerns and priorities of the Party and those of the majority of voters, including Labour's own 'heartlands'. As Gordon Brown is fond of saying, this was a time when the Labour Party resembled Shelley's description of his ailing grandmother: 'She had lost the art of communication but not alas the power of speech'.

Having famously been knocked over by the waves at his first conference as leader, Neil Kinnock gradually rolled back the tide of activist control, with the 1990 policy review being a critical moment. Kinnock also supported the then Party general secretary Larry Whitty in developing proposals for a national policy forum that would seek over time to replace adversarial resolutionary politics with a deliberative model of policy making. Despite the One Member One Vote drama and the first meeting of the policy forum, John Smith did not appear to have a grand plan to reform Party democracy. In contrast Tony Blair and the modernising enthusiasts around him saw the existing model of Party democracy as a sham and an impediment to electoral success. The New Labour transformation of party decision making had three elements. First, there was the successful attempt to recruit to the Party new members with opinions closer to those of the new leadership. Secondly, Blair innovated by holding full membership ballots on two key issues; clause IV and the pre-manifesto. Thirdly, and less well documented was a sophisticated and ruthless political management operation with operatives in all parts of the labour movement from constituency parties to trade unions and the youth and student wing. These measures gave Blair a level of control over his Party of which earlier leaders could only have dreamt. But it is also crucial to appreciate that Blair's control rested on consent: not only were most Labour members willing to accept any discipline as the price of victory but the left opposition to Blair was weak, divided and devoid of ideas.

After the 1997 Election, many in the New Labour hierarchy appeared to assume that command and control management of the Party could continue. The Partnership in Power reforms were seen mistakenly by both Blairites and the left as a further reduction in the capacity for dissent—a mistake which it took leadership defeats at conference 2000 to correct. More damagingly, New Labour's political machine appeared to forget the importance of consent. In Wales and London legitimacy was sacrificed to expediency and members came to see that their sovereignty depended on them agreeing with the leadership. By the conference of 2000 the style of Party policy making appeared to have returned to the 1970s, determined by last minute deals between the Party's leading politicians and the general secretaries of the country's largest trade unions.

The point about this brief history is that, in terms of both values and ideas and both amongst leaders and opposition groups, the pursuit of 'democracy' has always taken second place to the pursuit of power. Partnership in Power represented a real attempt to develop a new democratic model based upon a positive but realistic account of the role of Party members in holding leaders to account and determining future priorities (as one of its architects the author should declare an interest). But the model was initially rejected by the left because it appeared to make it more difficult to 'defeat' or 'mandate' the leadership, while it was insufficiently resourced by a sceptical Millbank and largely ignored by Ministers.

The Continuing Power of the Grassroots

If one argument against prioritising the democratic reform of parties as a route to civic renewal is that the formal model of party democracy is an illusion and the rhetoric dishonest, the other, paradoxically, is that leaders generally have to stay in touch with party grassroots. In this sense there is no problem with party democracy that needs to be fixed and thus no internal rationale for parties to reform. Put in highly simplified terms, the major parties appear to go through cycles of power, disillusionment, defeat, insularity, renewal and—usually—back to power. In the 1980s the perceived failure of Labour in office led to an increase in activist power. The need for Michael Foot then Neil Kinnock to keep a rebellious and assertive party on side meant Labour's leaders could not determine their policy agenda according to electoral needs. It was only with the defeat in 1992 that Labour's activists became willing to accept the primacy of electoral necessity in the determination of policy and presentation. Yet, after 1997 with Labour in power and inevitably disappointing some of the ambitions of its members, the Party becomes less compliant and leaders who thought they had thrown off for ever the need to pacify dissent and make deals with union bosses find themselves doing precisely this. The Conservatives are at a different stage of the cycle. Following the hollowing out and disillusionment of the Party under Major, William Hague lacks the authority to determine his policy and presentation by the desire to win a majority but must constantly reinforce his position by giving the Party what it wants. Arguably, it was the hostility of his Party that helped to see off his early attempt to brand himself as a socially liberal compassionate Conservative. It appears that it will take at least one more Tory defeat before its members, activists and representatives are willing to recognise or bend to electoral necessity. It is noteworthy that the decline of the Tory Party both in size and in significance as an institution in local communities has coincided with the gradual democratisation of the Party. The Tory Party was a considerably greater force in local communities when its leaders made absolutely no pretence of listening to members.

In summary, a number of factors require party leaders (whatever their opinions and inclinations) not to travel too far from grassroots opinions. Principal amongst these factors are the importance to the leaders' image of having support in the Party, the damage that can be done by internal dissent and the continuing need for at least a basic campaigning infrastructure on the ground.

The Limits to Parties as Community Champions

While some people may continue to believe that Labour need only return to resolutions and composites at conference to build a mass party, there is a more sophisticated version of the view that the internal reform of political parties can contribute significantly to broader political re-engagement. This is the attempt to turn local party organisation outwards, engaging with local people and becoming their champion. While a noble idea, there are several problems with this approach, two of which appear to be fatal.

First, while Party leaders may express enthusiasm about parties getting closer to communities this belies their desire to maximise discipline. Inevitably, the voice of local communities will tend to be loudest when opposing failure by public authorities (people rarely get active to express contentment). Only the most effective local activists and representatives would be able to mediate between the expectations of the public and the realities of power, and only then at propitious times. Secondly, it appears that community activists are increasingly unlikely to see political parties as the most fruitful channel for the pursuit of their interests. Generally, parties and their representatives are seen as part of the problem not the solution. Those involved in new forms of political activity on a national or international level may see themselves as being outside the political mainstream, organising in new ways precisely because traditional channels like political parties fail to articulate their demands. While at the neighbourhood level the involvement of political parties is often seen to endanger the claim of community activists to represent the whole community. Thus for many emerging political activists, parties are seen as either irrelevant, divisive or both.

Which takes us to the second view of the relationship between party, democracy and political renewal. Political parties continue to have a vital function in organising choices in elections and in ensuring that one element of political accountability relates to the pursuit of broad values. However, there is no question that the last four decades have seen the erosion of the social and cultural base of political parties. Such has been the decline in public support for parties as institutions that the authors of a major review of political disengagement in the developed democracies were able to conclude: 'The collapse of citizen engagement with political parties over the decades since [the 1970s] is as close to a universal generalisation as one can find in political science.'[3] The party affiliation model of loyalty to a single organisation seems not to fit the less deferential, more individualistic, faster changing realities of modern life. As David Walker states, commenting on work by Mair and van Biezen showing decline in party membership across Europe:[4] 'Party decline looks like it is part and parcel of a well-attested social phenomenon—the privatisation of our lives and retreat from the "public space". Parties are in the same empty place as trade unions and churches.'[5]

It is here there lies a possible key to the extent of popular political disengagement. For while the social, cultural and behavioural bases of parties have declined, the stranglehold which they have over the formal representative democratic process has—if anything—increased.

The Political Party Cartel

The party cartel—the monopoly over the representative democratic process held by the major parties—has many elements; but the following are perhaps the most important. Parties effectively control who can be elected to office locally, nationally and in the European Parliament. Although occasionally new parties appear to be breaking through (for example, the SDP in 1983 or the Greens in 1989) and equally occasionally exceptional individuals or circumstances produce electable independents (for example, Ken Livingstone, Martin Bell), in all other circumstances anyone who wants to be an elected representative in a local authority, assembly or Parliament must join and be nominated by one of the three major parties in England or the four major parties in Scotland and Wales.

Secondly, although it is a less direct and more variable process, it is parties that represent the first call on the accountability of politicians. The concept of political representation is contested, its definition elusive, its reality complex and varied. However, while MPs and councillors may ponder over whether they owe loyalty to their supporters, their electors or to certain groups within their electorate, the reality for the vast majority is that it is to their party that they must first and most completely be answerable. This accountability is downwards to their activists who must campaign for and re-select the candidate, but more powerfully upwards to the party hierarchy in party HQ, council executive or government: those whose patronage will determine the career prospects of the representative. Parties control not only entry to representative bodies, but also progression into the executives that control those bodies.

We have long grown used to the effect of party discipline on the power of parliament to call the executive to account. However, it is instructive to see the issue of party control in the light of the new arrangements for local

governance. The division of executive and scrutiny functions in local authorities requires that back bench councillors change their role in the council
chamber from that of committee fodder to the voice of the local community
calling the executive to account. In recognition of the way in which this whole
system could be undermined by party loyalty, Labour has changed its
standing orders so that the group whip cannot be applied to the scrutiny
function. But this move—welcome though it is—is likely to be of more
symbolic than real significance. In authorities run by their party, Labour
councillors will continue to be powerfully constrained by the patronage
powers of the executive and by the understandable desire not to embarrass
their own party in public. For this reason it will continue to be in party group
meetings rather than public scrutiny sessions that the executive will be called
to account by the majority group. As Colin Copus has written: 'It is clear that
the party group, and the discipline and loyalty that it expects and receives
from its members will see political decision-making and scrutiny remain
locked behind the doors of its private meetings—whatever political management model exists and whatever the political affiliations of those concerned.'[6]

A Reform Agenda

Political parties, despite their narrowing base and declining public legitimacy,
continue to control entry, progression and voice in the democratic representative process. But the argument here is not that we should do away with
parties. The party system is vital to ensuring that politics continues to be
based at least to some degree on choices between values and programmes. We
have only to look to Italy to see the danger that when traditional parties
decline the space can be filled by parties based on prejudice or personality.
But two processes must now be begun if the legitimacy of political parties is
not to become so weak as to threaten their place at the heart of our democratic
system.

The first of these two processes is that parties must be forced to adapt:
becoming more open, more broadly accountable and more genuinely representative. But we have to recognise that the case for party reform is not
usefully made either through appeal to some partisan notion of 'true party
democracy', or through the hope that parties will seek to balance their short
term electoral needs with a commitment to the overall health of the political
system. There may come a time when party reform of this kind may be
internally driven through a perception of enlightened self-interest, but this
will only happen when the clamour for reform coming from outside has
become too loud to ignore. This is why the second process should involve
governmental and constitutional reforms which have the effect of loosening
the party stranglehold on entry, progression and voice in the democratic
system.

In one area public concern has already driven Labour to move the debate
forward significantly. In subjecting party funding to legislation the Govern-

ment has taken an important step in recognising the relevance of party behaviour to the overall health of the political process. It is possible that over time controls on funding will require parties to put more emphasis on local communication than on expensive national publicity campaigns. In addition, rules about disclosure of major donations will at last subject the motives of rich benefactors to public scrutiny.

This addresses only one part of the problem. The still predominantly male, still overwhelmingly (in the case of the Conservatives and Liberal Democrats almost exclusively) white and increasingly aged profile of party members underlines the need to lower the barrier of party nomination for elected office. The process of party selection should move from one largely based on choosing the person in the party most suited to stand, to one based on identifying people in the community who share the broad values of the party and who have appropriate skills and/or strong community links—particularly with under-represented groups. The role of the party is not to act as a closed shop, but as an organisation that offers support to those in the community who share its broad values. This may appear to be a technical or even a semantic change. Indeed both the Conservatives and the Liberal Democrats already have more of a tradition of this kind of recruitment, but for Labour a shift of emphasis such as this would be of great significance. Crucially, the fact that the representative is more likely to have a base, networks, and skills outside the party will help to ameliorate the influence of the party on the representative in office. This is not to seek to abolish this influence—to do so would make representation on a party ticket meaningless—but it is to provide a better balance of influences and support networks; the party at the apex but not the party in exclusive control. In time—if reforms to parties halted or reversed the secular process of party disaffiliation—the move to a more inclusive form of selection (along the lines of American primaries) could be pursued.

These are some of the measures that might help to remove the party control over entry but reform is also needed to the primacy of internal party discipline and power in the processes of decision making and accountability in democratic institutions. There are many proposals to strengthen parliament in relation to the executive, most if not all of which would require (or enable) back-bench MPs to act in ways which cut across party lines to emphasise their collective scrutiny role, for example in select committees.[7] The scope for such reforms to affect the accountability of the executive is hinted at by the apparently better balance of power between executive and legislature in the Welsh Assembly and Scottish Parliament.

Focusing on local government, every party should be encouraged to follow Labour's lead and remove the whip from scrutiny. Beyond this parties should reinforce through exhortation, training and incentives that scrutinising the executive is a valued activity, even when it causes embarrassment to an executive of the same party. But a more radical step should also be considered, one that points to a wider constitutional agenda. Although there are bound to be tensions and problems, the relationship between Ken Livingstone and the members of the Greater London Authority appears to have great strengths in terms of the scope for and commitment to real scrutiny. This is surely not unrelated to the fact that Livingstone does not control the majority or even the largest (or even any) party group on the GLA. This is not to argue that future Mayors must not stand on a party ticket, but it points to the possible value of further extending the space between the domain of executive authority and that of legislative scrutiny. One possibility would be that the relationship between executive members (mayors or cabinet members) and the party group could become more like that between members and officers, with executives excluded from attending party group meetings or other party activities except within limits set by standing orders.

These reforms might go some way to reducing party control, and even renewing public confidence in parties as institutions capable of community representation. But the argument set out in this chapter points to the case for more fundamental constitutional reforms. It is unlikely that the attempt to reduce party control would be sufficient in itself to win the case for such reforms, but it could change the balance and content of long standing constitutional debates.

For example, proportional representation in its various forms could break up the major party cartel in a number of ways. First, by making it more possible for new parties to emerge, PR could threaten the existing parties' division of the political battle-ground. Secondly, by making party coalitions more necessary for power PR would make less likely control by a single party hierarchy over local or national executives. Thirdly, in an open list, multi-member constituency model, voters could have the capacity to select between different candidates providing citizens with more choice and offering those candidates who might lack leadership patronage a new and powerful source of legitimacy.

The questioning of party control also points to the case for a greater separation of powers. At the local level the electoral separation of executive and legislature/scrutiny body (currently available only in the case of directly elected mayors) could help to ensure that back-bench councillors are less easily dominated by executive members. In fact, such a separation would fit with the suggestion made earlier that parties be more open in the selection of candidates. If non-executive councillors no longer had a role in selecting the executive, nor were eligible themselves to join the executive, this would surely make more likely the possibility that parties would relax their control over the election of these councillors. Electing councillors whose role was exclusively to champion their locality and to call the executive to account would further undermine the already peculiar idea that parties should fight to the death to ensure every councillor is of their party. Indeed, unless parties did open up and loosen control, electors would rapidly come to recognise that party candidates were the least credible as genuine advocates of community interests and fearless challengers of the executive. There is increasingly disappointing feedback on the impact of the Government's current reforms. Thus, the imposition of separate elections for executive and non-executive, in combination with local party organisations having more freedom over who to select and who to support in non-executive elections, may now be the only viable route to the renewal of local governance.

Conclusion

Sadly, it is not the business of political parties to revive our political culture. To put it simply, any party would rather win on a 50 per cent turnout than lose on a 75 per cent turnout. The limited and self-interested ambitions that parties have in relation to democratic engagement as a whole is echoed in the partisan nature of most campaigns for greater 'democracy' within political parties. Hard though it is for a party loyalist like myself to admit it, parties are not part of the solution, they are at the heart of the problem. Despite important and legitimate concerns about the emergence of personality or single issue politics, it is time for those who are genuinely alarmed at the feebleness of representative democracy and its growing distance from the lives of ordinary people to demand action to lift the withering hand of party control from around the throat of our democratic system. Indeed, on reflection, it may be precisely our loyalty to our chosen political parties that has stood in the way of democrats mounting a more concerted campaign for the modernisation of our producerist political culture.

Notes

1 P. Smith, 'The Iron Law of Malarky', *Representation*, Vol. 37, No. 1 2000, pp. 60–4.
2 T. Ellis, 'Making the Iron Law Sensible', *Representation*, Vol. 37, No. 1 2000, pp 65–70.
3 R. D. Putnam, S. J. Pharr, & R. J. Dalton, 'Introduction', in S. J. Pharr, and R. D. Putnam, eds., *Disaffected Democracies*, New Jersey, Princeton, 2000.
4 P. Mair and van I. Biezen, 'Party members in 20 European democracies 1980–2000' in *Party Politics 7:1 2001*.
5 D. Walker, 'The party's over', *Guardian 16 Jan. 2001.*
6 C. Copus, 'The Party Group and Modernising Local Democracy' *Representation*, Vol. 36 No 3, pp. 243–50 .
7 G. Power, 'Creating a working Parliament', London, Hansard Society 2000.

Reforming the House of Commons

JOHN MAXTON, MP

THE establishment of the Scottish Parliament, the Welsh and London Assemblies, and the abolition of the hereditary peerages on their own represent the greatest constitutional change in a hundred years. Add changing constitutional links with the European Union, the further proposals for future reform of the House of Lords, the first use of voting by proportional representation for the new Parliament and Assemblies, the proposed referendum on the extension of proportional representation to the UK Parliament, and the first Blair Government becomes the most radical of the modern age.

At the same time, and much more profoundly, our society is being transformed by the most revolutionary period of technological change that the world has ever seen. Most of man's developments have taken place in the last five thousand years—a long time for people circumscribed by a life-span of 70 years but very short in the history of both mankind and, even more so, the world. In the last hundred years driven by technical and technological change our society has changed more than in the previous thousand years and in the past ten years that transformation has been even more rapid and there is little sign that the rate of change is slowing. Indeed it accelerates with every passing day. It is impossible to exaggerate the extent and importance of the revolution that has and is taking place. Anyone who doubts this has only to imagine how their great grandparents lived in 1900 and think of all the things they did not enjoy that we take for granted today.

That revolution has in most recent times been led by the changes in information technology and computers but is by no means confined to them. The rapid development of gene technology will probably give cures for many of the diseases that at present kill so many. It may even slow the ageing process allowing our children or at least our grandchildren to live to ages that we cannot comprehend. This will create enormous problems for societies whose processes are geared to life spans of 60–70 years. Even now we see the problems that the small increases in the average age that have already taken place pose for governments in health and pension provision. Genetically modified crops and food will allow us to feed many more in the world. No one could possibly argue against this taking place but the problems of an increasing world population this could cause must be faced.

Revolutionary Changes

It is in information technology, however, that the revolution has so far most affected our lives although often unseen. It is easy for all of us to use and appreciate the many machines and tools that make our lives so much more comfortable and enjoyable. It is much more difficult to understand how profoundly they are changing every aspect of our society at a speed that is almost impossible to comprehend. Man appears almost infinitely adaptable. This revolution has and will continue radically to alter the way in which we govern and are governed. The Internet already allows the electorate to know in great detail any action the Government takes. Television, radio and the print media give instant news of our politicians and their actions. Broadband technology will soon allow most of us to receive the Internet, and news from around the world on our television sets, our radios and our mobile phones. Undoubtedly we will use electronic voting in a general election in the very near future. This will end forever the interminable wait for the results that will decide the fate of the Government of the day. Voting, which may take place in supermarkets, even from your own home, will end at 10 p. m. and the result will be known minutes later.

The global economy that the information revolution has produced will impact more and more on our everyday lives. It is already raising important questions about how we are governed both nationally and internationally. International companies have to be enormous to survive. Some have con-siderably more wealth than small and even medium sized countries. Com-puters allow them to trade across national boundaries unseen and unhindered. All of us can now purchase goods and services from other countries avoiding taxation while we do so.

If governments can no longer control the national economy what role do they have? Is the development of supra-states like the European Union inevitable? Are even these large enough to protect its citizens from the worst aspects of globalisation? Will the new technologies like Genetically Modified crops allow us to feed the starving of the world?

Parliament Unchanged

In the midst of these constitutional and technological revolutions sits the House of Commons, the supposed centre of our democracy, making laws, which affect all of us. Yet this institution seems almost unaffected by the changes sweeping the rest of the country and world both constitutionally and technologically. In form and substance it appears stuck in a time warp somewhere in the middle of the 19th Century when the present building was built. Of course, there has been change. Some of the rules have been altered to make the hours that Members of Parliament work more reasonable. Some new technology has been introduced—usually too little, too late and too cheaply. But at its heart the House of Commons remains unchanged.

The style of the place both in the costumes worn by officials and the means of legislating remain as they were in the 19th Century. This cannot continue if the House is not to become an anachronism, a 'quaint' attraction for American tourists, historically interesting but of little relevance to the people it supposedly represents and within a modern democracy. Why hasn't it changed as so much else around it has? A series of 'conservative' Speakers who confused ancient customs with the 'rights of backbenchers' and the House's responsibility to hold the Government accountable have certainly not helped. Even now the new Speaker should call a Speaker's Conference to consider the future of the House of Commons.

Obviously its historical importance in the development of world democracy and the symbolic significance of the Houses of Parliament buildings themselves have made reform much more difficult than it would be in a more modern democracy. In a fast changing world tradition, however, has much less, if any, importance. Institutions that do not adapt themselves to the new world rightly die. If the House of Commons does not rapidly come to terms with that reality then it will cease to have any relevance.

Some important changes can be made quickly and within the context of the present building. Others demand more radical action. The first decision that has to be made must be to answer the question, 'What is the role of the House of Commons in a modern democracy?' First, it must both appear to represent the electorate who vote for it and actually do so. Secondly, it must ensure that proposed legislation is properly scrutinised. Thirdly, it must hold the Government to account for its actions. The first quick, least important but still relevant change, it can make is to its appearance. All 'fancy' costumes must be abolished, both by the Speaker and the officials of the House. The style of speaking must be changed. The Scottish Parliament and Welsh Assembly have shown that addressing each other by their proper names rather than by their constituencies makes them appear much more in tune with the modern world. In a country of many faiths and increasingly none, prayers conducted by one denomination of one set of beliefs is irrelevant at best and insulting at worst. The Speaker should simply walk into the Chamber from behind his Chair and start proceedings at the relevant time.

Does it matter that we abolish what seem to be ancient customs? To many it appears a side issue that diverts attention from the major reforms that are needed. If that were the case I would be on their side. However, if Parliament is to be modern and democratic it must appear to be so, as well as being so.

Needed Reforms

Many of the costumes and customs were designed to symbolise authority, to make those who govern different from those who are governed. They emphasise the absurd anomaly that we remain in this country, subjects of the monarch and not citizens of our own democracy. And they are changes that can be made quickly and cheaply. They would show that Parliament was determined to change itself in other ways.

The useful changes that have been made in the hours the House sits must be continued. While a nine to five, four day week may not be desirable, something close to it must be the aim. If we are to encourage more young women and men of all walks of life to be part of the democratic process and seek to be Members of Parliament, then we must have hours that are more suitable to their needs. However, we must not see changing hours as the only reform that matters.

There are those who argue that every reduction in the hours that the House sits is a reduction in the ability of backbenchers to properly scrutinise legislation and to hold the executive to account. How many pieces of legislation have been radically altered or how many government actions have been truly challenged by sitting for long tedious hours in the House or on Committees? Very few. The House only has power when the electorate has decided that no single Party shall have a majority in the House of Commons. The best way of properly scrutinising legislation, as I hope to show later, is to give Members of Parliament the proper tools and powers to do the job. Little is gained by keeping everyone out of his or her bed for long wearisome hours.

If legislation is to be more rigorously scrutinised and better informed, then a proper process of pre-legislative scrutiny must be instituted. This would entail Members being appointed to a Departmental Committee of some size. From that Committee would be drawn Committees to consider proposals for legislation presented by the Ministers in that Department. That Committee would call witnesses before it to consider how that legislation would impact on those it would affect, as well as finding out whether the proposals made sense to experts in the field, and getting the views of any organisations interested or campaigning in that area. Having completed their inquiry, they would then present a Report to the Department who would take account of its findings when drafting their legislation. The Members who were part of the scrutiny committee would also form the Standing Committee to consider the Bill presented by the Ministers in detail.

If this necessary reform is introduced, than it is essential that the annual sessions of Parliament be abolished as well. Each year the Parliamentary session begins in November with the Queen's Speech, during which the monarch informs Members of the House of Commons (including the Prime Minister and his Cabinet) what legislation the Government, elected by the people of the country, is going to introduce in that session.

A Government that has been elected by the people of Britain on a proposed programme of legislation should have the whole period of the Parliament to introduce that legislation. If it is to be scrutinised as suggested above, then it would be difficult to complete major Bills in the eleven months at present available.

If necessary at all there should be one opening of Parliament and one Queen's Speech immediately after the election, when the Government will lay out its legislative programme for the Parliament and then have the next four/ five years to implement it. If necessary, the Prime Minister could present an annual report to Parliament in October in which he/she could spell out the changes to the programme that are being proposed and what extra legislation the Government considers necessary.

It is a strange anomaly in a modern democracy that an unelected hereditary monarch tells the elected representatives what they are going to do in the next twelve months. Whatever one's view of having a monarch as head of state, it must be wrong for an unelected person to play such a role in a democracy. It again emphasises that we remain subjects and not citizens and that the Government is styled Her Majesty's Government, not the People's Government.

Ending the sessional rules would also allow for better planning of the parliamentary year and the abolition of the long summer recess. After all, it was introduced to allow Members of Parliament to escape the disease-ridden capital during the long, hot summer months of the 18th Century! Like any other people, MPs are entitled to holidays; but all of them do not have to be present to ensure that business is carried out. There is no reason why Parliament should not sit for most of the year with only short statutory breaks at the same time as everybody else.

There have been moves to timetable many more pieces of legislation to ensure that proper debate within time scales that are reasonable can take place. It is now time to timetable all legislation. Thus the work of Parliament can be properly planned and Members can know when they can work in their constituencies, when they have to be in Parliament, and when they can go on holiday with their families. Again, the traditionalists will argue that this reduces the ability of backbenchers to hold the Government to account and will reduce the time given to properly scrutinise legislation. As with the House of Commons, debating abstruse points for long hours on Committee does nothing to improve the quality of legislation or rarely to change it.

If the House of Commons is to represent its electorate properly and hold the executive to account, then it must have greater powers to insist that the executive give it the information it wishes. At present the Speaker has no power to insist that Ministers make statements to the House of Commons. The Speaker should have such powers. Select Committees cannot insist that Ministers appear before them to give evidence. In most cases they do, but it is at their pleasure, not the Committees'. While there may be occasions when sensitive information should not be made public, that does not mean that Members of Parliament should not receive it. The Freedom of Information Act has started the process of ending the culture of secrecy that has dogged British governments for far too long, but more must be done. In a modern democracy, citizens are entitled to the information they require to make decisions both about their own lives and about the government they wish to elect.

All of these changes would make the House of Commons more representative, more in tune with the 21st Century, give better scrutiny to legislation, and hold the executive to better account. All of them could and should be implemented without major changes in the present structures of the House of Commons itself. However they do not bring the institution into the modern world of information rich technology.

Technology and Reform

In the age of the computer it still takes 15 minutes to complete each vote in the House of Commons, which is recorded by all Members trooping through two different lobbies. In October 2000 when it took six hours to elect a new Speaker, one and a half hours were taken up with going through the voting lobbies. The House of Commons should introduce electronic voting as soon as possible to avoid the derision that this anachronism produces among our electorate and other Parliamentarians around the world, who use electronic voting with no apparent problems. Traditionalists argue that this is the only time to meet Ministers and discuss issues with them. Some modernisers believe that electronic voting could be organised in such a way that that would not be lost. Others believe that the time wasted by such an archaic voting system is not balanced by any perceived benefits.

From time immemorial, all governments have used secrecy as a tool of power. They know and the people don't. That has allowed governments to make decisions and tell the governed that, as they do not know the facts, they are not capable of being involved in that decision-making. That has been equally true of the representatives of the people. Too often Members of Parliament have not been able to obtain the information they require properly to question the actions of government at the time and at the speed that makes it relevant. Modern technology should stop this from happening. All government departments maintain web sites on the Internet that allow anyone to access information about the Government. The House of Commons, too, maintains a very good web site that allows anyone to read the Hansard Debates, Committee Reports and the future business of the House.

The Government can speak directly to the people of the country both through the Internet and more generally through television and radio. They have no need to tell the Members of Parliament, and rely on them to tell their constituents what is happening. Parliament complains that important government announcements are made through the media rather than to it. The Prime Minister can be asked questions on television by ordinary members of the public as well as being questioned by Members of Parliament in the House of Commons. These are already possible and happening. Technologically smart card and voice-activated devices will allow us to vote from home, not just in general elections, but in instant referendums on whatever policy the Government wishes to put before the people. Digital compression will allow increasingly larger and larger amounts of information to be transmitted through a variety of media.

The lines between complete participatory democracy and representative democracy will be blurred. Governments can speak directly to the people and ask them for their opinion instantly. Instant decisions given after limited one-sided arguments are not the best way to run a democratic state. Representatives elected to bring mature and thoughtful judgment should take the decisive decisions, hold the Government to account, represent minorities as well as majorities, and ensure that their constituents are protected from both public and private bureaucracy.

Those who believe, however, in representative democracy must use the new technologies to ensure that they offer proper scrutiny of legislation, provide fast efficient services to their electorate and have the same information as government departments in order to hold them to account. If they cling to the present practices in the name of tradition, then any Government of whatever persuasion will ignore them and talk directly to the people, using all the options open to them.

Each Member of Parliament should have an office both within Parliament and within his/her constituency which has the most modern proven technology. Fast broadband internet connections between the offices and into government departments, both local and national, must be the norm. Video conferencing facilities must be available to allow the Members to talk to staff and constituents whenever required. As voice e-mail becomes more readily available then it, too, should be a normal part of every MP's office. Members will have to become accustomed to dealing with constituents' problems almost instantaneously. Taking an e-mail or video call, contacting the relevant government department, expecting a reply back by e-mail within hours, and then informing the person of the outcome.

More and more documents will be found and read on screen. More and more Bills and Acts will be held on the Intranet, instantly available to members and the general public. More and more reports will be in such electronic form that they can be 'searched' for those parts most relevant to a Member's interests. Each Committee Room within the parliamentary estate must be technologically viable. Every seat must have a screen terminal linked into the Intranet. When a Committee sits, a Member will personalise the screen at his seat, using his smart card identifier. This will contain either eye or finger print recognition, so that only the Member to whom it refers will be able to use it. (This will be essential when electronic voting is introduced in the House of Commons itself.)

Members scrutinising legislation will thus have instant access to the legislation, amendments, previous Hansards, Government policy documents, briefs sent to them electronically by both individual constituents and pressure groups concerned with the proposed legislation. As each of these can be 'searched' electronically, Members will be able to find any required information quickly and efficiently. This gives a capacity to challenge Ministers with knowledge and speed, something which is just not possible at the moment.

Ministers, too, will be linked electronically to their offices. Instead of 5–10 civil servants sitting in the Committee Room, ready to give advice to the Minister when required, one will be sitting at a desk in the department, feeding answers to questions directly onto the Minister's screen. How much more efficient this will be! Much more importantly, it gives both sides the information upon which rational debate can then take place. The debating chamber itself must be equipped with the same Intranet screens as committee rooms, so that Members can call up information as they require it during debates. It is not sufficient that such technology be available to Members: now their offices, committee rooms and the debating chamber must be designed to ensure that as new technology becomes available, the rooms can be quickly adapted to its use.

Cloud Cuckooland?

By now most readers and particularly constitutional traditionalists will be whispering phrases like 'cloud cuckooland', 'stark raving madness', 'the end of British democracy', etc. etc. But if representational democracy is to survive, let alone flourish, then the House of Commons must change quickly. It is not a matter of setting up a Committee to examine proposals and five years later coming back with half-hearted, watered down compromises. Action on at least some of this must be immediate. If not, the Government will have increasing freedom to speak directly to the people and ignore more and more an ill-informed, traditional House of Commons.

The most important decision that must be taken with proper care but with some speed is the future of the Houses of Parliament themselves. Put simply, buildings designed for gas lighting and horse drawn carriages are totally unsuitable for the sort of democratic parliament I describe above. The best offices are outside the main building. It is taking years to lay cable, because the 'ancient' fabric of the building cannot be disturbed. By the time it is laid it is out of date and in need of replacement. A Speaker's Conference should consider urgently the need to build or find new premises that will be modern and adaptable. There are those who believe that this will consign Parliament to some modern, anonymous concrete office block. The latest parliamentary building and the Dome show that new buildings can be exciting and stylish. Properly designed they can become as symbolic as the present parliamentary buildings.

Of course, such a building will be expensive. However, there is no need for it to be in central London. Although it would be sacrilege to sell the Houses of Parliament themselves, the new, recently built or developed buildings that make up the rest of the extensive parliamentary estate could be sold. They are very desirable real estate in the centre of a vibrant capital city. Their sale would go a long way to off-set the costs of building a new Parliament elsewhere. The symbolic Houses of Parliament could be turned into a World Heritage site for Democracy, a major tourist attraction bringing much needed revenue to London and maybe providing some of the revenue costs for the new Parliament.

Will any of this ever happen? I believe it must if democracy as we know it is to survive. If none of it happens then, given devolution and the development of a wider, more democratic European Union, there is a real danger that the UK Parliament will become an insignificant backwater, a quaint tourist attraction with little power, ignored by both the electors and the Government of the day.

Will Scottish Devolution Make a Difference?

JOYCE McMILLAN

OF all the elements of the Labour Government's constitutional reform programme, Scottish devolution is the one which should, given its history, have the most obvious bearing on any debate about a new culture of citizenship for the 21st century. There is, of course, a certain element of truth in the *realpolitik* view that the Scottish Parliament exists today purely because of the electoral pressure exerted on Scottish Labour since the 1970s by an increasingly successful and credible Scottish National Party. But if electoral imperatives provided the raw political motive for change, it is also undeniable that the final, successful phase of the hundred-year struggle for Scottish home rule—the phase between the founding of the Scottish Constitutional Convention in 1988, and the election of parliament in 1999—had its roots in a much more widespread civic revolt against the ethos and policies of the UK governments of the 1980s. It was a movement that found various voices in different parts of the UK, notably in the work of Charter 88; Scots were by no means alone in reacting against the exaggerated secrecy and centralism of those governments, their brutal first-past-the-post majoritarianism, their deeply un-Conservative insensitivity to the political and cultural diversity of the UK, their curiously 'retro' form of British nationalism, and the ideological absolutism with which they embraced what many saw as a blatantly reactionary political project.

In Scotland, however, the civic revolt found its focus in the idea of creating a new parliament for Scotland, one that would not only, in a simple sense, give a democratic voice to the nation, but would also—in the words of a much-read pamphlet of the period by Bernard Crick and David Miller[1]—have the opportunity to become a 'model of democracy' for the 21st century, exploring new methods of consultation, participation and consensus-building, committing itself wholeheartedly to the idea of plural and multi-layered democracy in Europe, and helping to develop a strong new relationship between citizens and government that might survive the pressures of the new millennium. Culturally, the movement was much influenced both by models of multi-layer democracy elsewhere in the European Union, notably in Spain and Germany, and by the world-shaking events in central and eastern Europe that took place shortly after the founding of the Convention in 1988. Just as Charter 88 consciously modelled itself on the example of the Czech civic dissidents of Charter 77, so many Scots close to the work of the Convention were inspired by the vision of a new value-based human politics put forward by civil society thinkers like Vaclav Havel at the time of the 1989 'velvet

Published by Blackwell Publishers, 108 Cowley Road, Oxford OX4 1JF, UK and 350 Main Street, Malden, MA 02148, USA

revolutions'. Above all, the Scottish home rule movement of the Nineties saw itself as enlightened, outward-looking and internationalist in approach, as opposed to the warm beer nostalgia-mongers of the then British government.

So it was hardly surprising that when the new British government, following the positive referendum result of September 1997, set about drafting the devolution legislation and preparing the ground-rules for the Scottish Parliament, the overwhelming view of those who took part in the debate was that they wanted something radically different from Westminster, with its thumping majorities, its fierce adversarial culture, its camp ceremonial traditions, and its famous atmosphere of a gentlemen's club patronised by rowdy public schoolboys. It is true that some of these aspirations towards a new style of politics were as vague as they were idealistic, and almost inevitably doomed to disappointment. One professional body which submitted its views to the government's Consultative Steering Group (CSG) on the Parliament during 1998 said that it hoped for 'a caring parliament' whose members would be 'free from self-interest'; almost all said that they wanted to see a parliament with an open and consensual ethos, avoiding Westminster-style confrontation and point-scoring.[2] But while practical proposals for achieving this ideal parliament were thin on the ground, the strength and consistency of feeling on these issues revealed both the extraordinary level of disaffection from Westminster as a useful form of public forum, and the extent to which the idea of the new Scottish Parliament had created one of those rare moments in politics when people raise their eyes to a wider horizon, and give expression, however briefly, to some of their deepest hopes and dreams about how an ideal political system might work.

The Scotland Act

The final scheme for the Scottish parliament, as enshrined in the Scotland Act of 1998 and in the CSG's report *Shaping Scotland's Parliament* (formally adopted by the Parliament itself soon after its election), therefore contained many provisions which tended to shift the new Scottish institutions, albeit modestly, in the direction suggested by the work of the Constitutional Convention and by the CSG consultations. The political skill and intense commitment of Donald Dewar was important in overcoming the doubts of Cabinet colleagues about this most innovative Act. Most strikingly, the parliament was to be elected by an additional member system of proportional representation, which would deny an overall majority to any single party. There were, of course, many pragmatic reasons for the Labour Party's original decision to support a proportional system, taken in the Constitutional Convention shortly after the 1992 election. But the survival of the PR scheme into legislation, following Labour's massive 1997 election victory, certainly owes something to the sheer weight of public and civic opinion in Scotland against any suggestion of another first-past-the-post parliament, with its colossal false majorities, and its radical exclusion of minority opinion. This shift away from first-past-the-post majoritarian government represents, in itself, a massive break with Westminster culture. As Robert Hazell argues in the recent Constitution Unit survey *The State and the Nations*,[3] the most striking difference of atmosphere between Westminster and the Scottish Parliament lies precisely in what is absent at Holyrood, namely the self-deluding triumphalism of majority governments blinded by the electoral system to the modest levels of their actual support among voters.

The parliament was also set up to achieve a stronger ethos of inclusion and participation in at least four other significant ways. The subject-based committees of the Scottish Parliament were given an exceptionally wide range of powers and responsibilities, including a duty to explore innovative and effective new methods of consultation, to travel throughout Scotland as part of that consultative process, to play a major and early role in scrutinising and refining legislative proposals, to mount wide-ranging investigations into the proper administration of policy, and to initiate legislation in areas of concern where the Executive is not prepared to act. There was a spectacular push, at least within the Labour Party, to achieve gender balance in the parliament by 'twinning' winnable constituencies, and 'zipping' the additional member party lists; the result is a Scottish parliament which is almost 38 per cent female, the third highest figure in Europe. There was a battery of smaller measures to allow individual citizens to petition and interact with parliament in a more satisfactory way than has been traditional at Westminster. And there was much discussion of the potential for using new technology both as a tool for civic education, and to set up imaginative new lines of communication between the parliament and communities across Scotland, through the use of terminals in libraries, schools, village halls and so on.

A Parliament With a Mission

In other words, if ever a parliament was set up with an overt mission to encourage a new culture of citizenship and participation, the Scottish Parliament of 1999 was that body; and the failures and successes of its first eighteen months of operation therefore carry an unusually high level of significance for those interested in contemporary citizenship issues.

This for six broad reasons. First, on the positive side, there is no doubt that the committee system of the new parliament has already won widespread respect and support, and is playing a significant role in examining previously under-scrutinised areas of Scottish government. It has been argued, for example, that the Education, Culture and Sport Committee, chaired by Labour MSP Mary Mulligan, played an exemplary role during the Scottish Qualifications Authority scandal of Summer 2000, announcing an immediate wide-ranging inquiry while Executive ministers were still denying any major problems, and conducting that inquiry not only with persistence, integrity, and powerful cross-party consensus, but also with some political flair; the committee certainly achieved some of the most positive media coverage of the Scottish Parliament's short history when it visited Lanarkshire to take live evidence, in front of the cameras, from young people traumatised by the chaos surrounding last year's examination results.[4] The Enterprise and Life-long Learning Committee, chaired by John Swinney until he became SNP leader in autumn 2000, has also been welcomed as a model of constructive and creative cross-party working.[5]

Secondly, it is already clear that the development of a more plural system of democracy in the UK is creating the potential for more diversity in policy-making, for a more creative exchange of best practice, and for a more flexible and genuinely consultative political culture in which policy decisions can sometimes be revised without the government being shot down in flames. Prime examples so far include Scotland's famous 'Cubie' compromise on student tuition fees, reached at the insistence of Labour's Liberal Democrat partners in the Scottish Executive (and already being eyed with interest by the devolved administration in Northern Ireland); and the recent hints by Scottish First Minister Henry McLeish—under pressure from a powerful consensual report by the Scottish Parliament's Health Committee—that ways are being sought of implementing in Scotland the Sutherland Report on long-term care of the elderly. There has also been a cross-party attempt—welcomed by campaigning groups across the UK—to raise the issue of whether Scotland might be able, within its own jurisdiction and local authorities, to avoid implementing some of the more unpleasant aspects of the government's asylum and refugee regime.

In the third place, the Scottish parliament has established itself with surprising speed as the main focus of Scotland's political life and its main forum for debate, even among groups previously hostile. Essentially, the parliament's devolved responsibilities include most of the key 'bread and butter' issues—health, education, many aspects of transport and employ-ment—about which voters say they care. In the first eighteen months of the parliament's operation, reporting of Westminster in the Scottish media was almost entirely eclipsed by coverage of the Scottish Parliament, both positive and negative. As one observer put it, if the relationship between the modern citizen and political institutions is that of the dog to the lamp-post, then the Scottish Parliament has rapidly become the lamp-post of choice for most Scots. This intense early focus on the Scottish Parliament is likely to correct itself a little as the next Westminster general election begins to dominate the news agenda. But as David McCrone pointed out in the Summer 2000 issue of *Scottish Affairs*,[6] a poll conducted by ICM for Scotland on Sunday in January 2000 found that 51 per cent of Scots interviewed saw the Scottish Parliament as the most important body determining their future, compared with only 31 per cent who saw Westminster in that light. In simple terms, it seems that the Scottish Parliament's status as a legislature geographically and culturally closer to the people, more accurately representative of their views, and responsible for most key social issues, has given it a powerful head start in terms of public attention and feelings of 'ownership'; the question is whether that advantage can be maintained, or will give way to increasing alienation.

Fourthly, according to a Spring 2000 survey by John Curtice of Strathclyde University,[7] the Scottish Parliament's electoral system has gained widespread acceptance as fairer and more appropriate than a first-past-the-post system. This is not to say that the AMS system is not criticised; some commentators regularly mock it as a bizarre un-British innovation. But despite this widespread 'disavowal' of the system, few can be found who actually want to revert to first-past-the-post for the Scottish Parliament; on the contrary, the main pressure, at least from the public, seems to be for a further radicalisation of the system towards 'open' party lists, ordered by voters at election time. The electoral system has been particularly important by preventing the kind of crude majoritarian culture referred to by Robert Hazell above; it maintains consent to the Parliament by giving all parties a stake in it, by allowing the representation of significant minorities (the Scottish Green Party and Scottish Socialists), and in guaranteeing support from those areas of Scotland outside the central belt which traditionally feared a parliament dominated by the huge Labour majorities of west central Scotland.

Fifth, the presence of a large group of women in the Scottish parliament has had a major—if unquantifiable—positive impact on the atmosphere of the institution, which looks, broadly speaking, much more like a normal modern working environment than the rowdy Commons. Any observer who spends much time watching Scottish parliamentary committees at work, or listening to the detail of policy debates, is bound to be struck by how seriously many of the parliament's female members take the commitment to creating a new style of politics. They may not always be able, under party pressures, to put these ideals fully into practice, but many of them seem acutely conscious of grassroots pressure to work in a more practical, problem-solving way, and to avoid pointless party confrontation.

It should be noted that women MSPs suffered some astonishing media abuse in the first months of the Parliament. Some commentators seemed almost unable to contain their fear and loathing at the sight of a legislature that included so many ordinary Scottish women, and produced bizarre tirades of personal abuse about their alleged fatness, ugliness, stupidity, absurdity, unfitness for office, and excessive Scottishness of voice. But eighteen months on, this strange outburst seems, with hindsight, almost like the death-rattle of an old political order unable to believe that its last hour had come. The presence of the women no longer attracts much comment in the Scottish media. The main concern is that the parliament should not blot its copy-book, come the next election in 2003, by allowing its level of female representation to slip; and it is regrettable that on this as on so many other matters, the London media tend, lazily or economically, to take their news from the anti-devolution Scottish press.

Then finally, there is the persistence, around the Scottish parliament, of some fairly strong and proactive forces of civil society. Unpublished research at Edinburgh University[8] suggests that Scottish civil society organisations such as professional associations, trade unions, churches, environmental and anti-poverty pressure-groups, women's organisations and some community groups, are already among the most satisfied 'customers' of the Scottish Parliament, although they may have more reservations about the more traditional operation of the Scottish Executive. They report ample opportunities to give evidence to committees, a sense that serious points made are being taken on board wherever possible, and excellent feedback on the use made of their evidence, so that a strong continuing loop of communication is established.

In 1999, in addition, the Scottish Executive allocated funds to support the development of a Scottish Civic Forum, based on the old Civic Assembly that grew up alongside the Constitutional Convention to discuss wider social and economic issues; despite strained finances and a chronically low public profile, the Forum has attracted some 300 member organisations across the spectrum of Scottish civic life, and is working hard to establish itself as a useful channel of communication between Scottish civil society, the Parliament and Executive. And towards the end of 2000, the journalist and publisher Kenneth Roy launched an interesting initiative in the form of an independent Institute for Contemporary Scotland, designed to parallel and reflect on the development of Scotland's formal political institutions, self-financed by 500 founder members, eminent Scots each paying £250 as an initial donation. Civic Scotland, in other words—the wider community of concerned and active citizens that found its voice in the Constitutional Convention—remains a powerful if sometimes elusive presence on the political scene; and it is well placed to develop a strong consultative relationship with the new institutions it helped create, both through individual groups and organisations, and through wider umbrella bodies.

Problems None-the-less

On the negative side, however, there is substantial evidence of disillusionment and disappointment with the new devolved institutions among Scottish voters. In a System Three poll for *The Herald* (Glasgow) in June 2000, only 27 per cent of those interviewed said that their view of the parliament was broadly favourable, compared with 57 per cent whose view was unfavourable; and in February 2000 a poll for *The Scotsman* found that a total of 91 per cent of Scots said that the parliament had done only 'a little' (64 per cent) or 'nothing' (27 per cent) for the country . The caveat should be added that this pattern of disappointment with the performance of the parliament does not seem to have eroded support for its existence. On the contrary, the most widespread feeling seems to be that the constitutional change has not been radical enough; in April 2000, for example, a System Three poll found an astonishing 62 per cent of Scots agreeing that the Parliament should have more powers, and only 8 per cent inclined to think that its powers should be reduced.

In terms of the parliament's failures, one of the most important, in public perception, seems to lie in the persistence within the parliament of a strong party system which voters increasingly dislike, and with which they do not identify. Throughout the UK, voters are increasingly inclined to ask politicians whether they tend to act on their principles and conscience, or simply to toe the party line. In the new Scottish Parliament, that question comes with an added nationalist twist: not only whether MSPs intend to serve their constituents before their party leaders, but whether they intend to vote in the interests of Scotland, or in the interests of London-based party leaderships. The depth of the mistrust of modern party politics is obvious both in the unpopularity of the 'closed list' element of the AMS electoral system—voters clearly dislike the idea of party leaderships choosing which potential MSPs will top the lists—and by the exceptional popularity, indeed the near-celebrity status, of the three 'independent' members of the parliament, the Scottish Socialist Tommy Sheridan, the Green Party representative Robin Harper, and the Labour rebel Denis Canavan. Indeed, when Canavan briefly flirted, following Henry McLeish's election as Labour leader in October 2000, with the idea of returning to Labour, he was subjected to such a barrage of abuse in the letters pages of the Scottish press that he rapidly backed off, and carried through his earlier threat to resign his Westminster parliamentary seat. Of course, the problem of the growing unpopularity of political parties is a pervasive one across the west. But as we have seen, for a brief moment between 1997 and 1999, many Scots allowed themselves to dream of a parliament in which party loyalties would be laid aside, and parliamentarians would work selflessly together for the good of all the people. And the genuine moves towards greater cross-party co-operation and a less adversarial culture which have been made in the parliament have not been enough to prevent disappointment, or gleeful weekly newspaper headlines hailing the return to dirty political business as usual.

Nor has this been the only source of bitter disappointment. The abject failure of the parties to secure the election of a single black or Asian ethnic minority representative to the parliament dealt a serious blow, right at the outset, to the parliament's claims to represent a new, inclusive Scotland based on civic rather than ethnic values. There is also a sense of tension and disappointment surrounding the parliament's relationship with the Scottish Executive, which still retains much of the same personnel and ethos as the old mandarin Scottish Office, and whose officials remain part of the UK Civil Service.

In essence, the devolution process has so far been a partial revolution, with the Scottish Parliament often genuinely engaged on developing a new and more open relationship with the people, Scottish Executive officials attempting a kind of hyper-consultative update of their methods without surrendering power or changing their fundamental management style, and Executive ministers caught in the crossfire. As a result, one of the themes of the parliament's first year was a recurring complaint from the civil service about the number of questions MSPs were asking, as if they had somehow been surprised to find that 129 new MSPs, charged with the full-time job of improving the government of Scotland, were subjecting their work to much closer examination; and the row over parliamentary questions was simply the tip of an iceberg of issues concerning the appropriate administration and servicing of the new structures of Scottish government, in a climate where voters are easily persuaded that extra money spent on democratic institutions is simply money down the drain.[9]

New Parliament in a Cold (Ideological) Climate

For in the end, most of the major failures of the new Parliament and Executive, as catalysts for a new culture of civic participation, have had more to do with general problems facing political institutions in affluent western societies today, than with issues specific to Scotland or the UK. The sense of disappointment with the parliament, for instance, is not only about specific failures to challenge the traditional pattern of British party politics, but about the chronic mismatch, in millennial politics, between voters' expectations of what national governments can do for them—particularly in a context of national renewal at a cultural and symbolic level—and the restricted room for manoeuvre they actually enjoy. In that sense, the present Scottish political scene carries faint echoes of similar experiences during the Nineties in east and central Europe.

Similarly, there is a feeling that the Parliament has not fulfilled its promise to use new technology to reach out to the people in radical ways; but this has less to do with the performance of the Parliament's information programme— which has created an excellent interactive website, put all MSPs on line and on e-mail, and generated a huge, well-organised and easily accessible archive of electronic information about the parliament's work—than with the intrinsically diffuse and private nature of electronic communications, which simply lack the strong collective and social impact of traditional media such as mass rallies, BBC interviews and phone-ins, or letters to the press.

Above all, the generally negative view of the Parliament expressed in opinion polls clearly owes as much to the pervasive late-20th-century prejudice against politicians and their activities as to any specific failings of the Scottish Parliament itself. Ever since the rise of neo-liberal and anti-state ideology in the 1970s, we have been living in an age in which the arguments for government have largely been forgotten, and the arguments against government endlessly repeated. At the same time, consumer choice has been elevated to a new status as our most important means of expressing ourselves and shaping our futures, and politics reduced to a kind of spectator sport or branch of show business, which we are encouraged to watch and mock as passive consumers in front of the telly, rather than to embrace as a part of our lives for which we share responsibility.

The cultural pervasiveness of this view, combined with the fact that large swathes of the English-language media are in the hands of owners and editors committed to extreme neo-liberal and economistic views, almost guarantees a rough ride to any new democratic institution—particularly one with any radical ideas about citizenship and participation—emerging in the English-speaking world today. In its first year, the Scottish Parliament received almost unremittingly hostile and contemptuous coverage from *The Scotsman* and *Scotland on Sunday*, from the leading Scottish tabloid *The Daily Record*, and from the Scottish editions of the *Daily Telegraph*, still widely read among Scottish Conservatives. This reached its peak early in 2000 in the *Daily Record's* unpredictable decision to mount a savage campaign of opposition—supported by the private referendum plans and massive national poster campaign of Stagecoach millionaire Brian Souter—to the Scottish Executive's plan to repeal the notorious Section 28 legislation on the 'promotion' of homosexuality in schools, known in Scotland as Section 2a. To its massive credit, and despite repeated media attempts to portray the Executive and Parliament as 'split' or 'wavering' on the issue, the Parliament never flinched from its five-to-one majority in favour of the repeal. Indeed, its set-piece debate on the repeal produced perhaps the most compassionate, intelligent and well-informed discussion on the Section 28 controversy ever staged in a British democratic forum.

However, in creating such a cruel travesty of a grass-roots citizen campaign, in whipping up massive opinion poll majorities against the repeal through systematic disinformation, and in hijacking the language of participation and 'listening government' for crudely reactionary ends supported by the outlay of massive personal wealth, Brian Souter and the *Daily Record's* then editor, Martin Clarke, staged a pyrotechnic display of how vulnerable the democratic institutions of a small country can be to the might of major media companies determined to discredit them, and to influence individuals who can afford to buy political power. The Scottish Parliament withstood the pressure this time; but a huge swathe of Scotland's tabloid-reading public was left with an enduring, deeply damaging and almost entirely false impression of an elitist parliament that 'did not listen' to the voice of the people.

Contrary Forces

The devolution process in Scotland should therefore be seen as an important and fascinating site of struggle between those forces pushing towards a new culture of citizenship for the 21st century, and those forces in society, the media and economy which militate strongly against it. Among those who are active citizens and who see themselves as such, who are in a position to give evidence to parliamentary committees, to attend debates, to find out how the system works, to take part in executive consultations, to digest the serious and extensive coverage of parliamentary affairs available on radio and television and in sections of the broadsheet press, and to play their full role in the civic process, the Parliament is popular, strongly supported, far more accessible and clearly focussed on practical concerns than Westminster could ever have been, and is widely perceived as a success.

However, among the majority who have no such direct contact with the political process—and who might well, in the long working-hours culture of millennial Britain, have difficulty in finding time to be active citizens even if the opportunity was offered directly to them—the surge of excitement and hope surrounding the new institution has already proved a rapidly wasting asset, vulnerable both to the general culture of political apathy and cynicism and to the specific attacks of a hostile media, modified only by a stubborn gut nationalism which would not wish to see Scotland's parliament abolished. Unless the Scottish Parliament sticks boldly to its reform and participation agenda, in other words unless it finds increasingly innovative ways of directly involving those who are not already 'active citizens', resolutely confronts the real and formidable socio-economic obstacles to a new culture of participation, develops new networks of communication to marginalise hostile media, and identifies new ways of generating effective and widely-supported policy in the key areas of social welfare devolved to it, then it could soon become as discredited as most other elected governments in our post-political age; and as cynically disregarded, in the great rush to the supermarket that has become the defining political act of our time.

Acknowledgement

* I would like to record special thanks to Lindsay Paterson, Professor of Education Policy at the University of Edinburgh, for his advice and support in preparing this essay.

Notes

1 Bernard Crick and David Miller, *To Make the Parliament of Scotland a Model For Democracy*, Edinburgh, John Wheatley Centre, 1996 .
2 Scottish Office, *Shaping Scotland's Parliament: the Report of the Consultative Steering Group on the Scottish Parliament*, Edinburgh, The Stationery Office, 1999, Annexes D and E.
3 Robert Hazell, ed., *The State and the Nations: the First Year of Devolution in the United Kingdom*, The Constitution Unit/Imprint Academic, 2000, p. 10.
4 Lindsay Paterson, *Crisis in the Classroom*, Edinburgh, Mainstream Publishing, 2000.
5 Comprehensive information about the work of the Scottish Parliament, including committee reports, minutes, evidence etc., at the Scottish Parliament website, www.scottish.parliament.uk.
6 David McCrone, 'Opinion Polls in Scotland: May 1999–June 2000', *Scottish Affairs* No. 32, Summer 2000, pp. 86–94.
7 John Curtice, Ben Seyd, Alison Park, Katarina Thomson, 'Wise After the Event?

Attitudes to Voting Reform following the 1999 Scottish and Welsh Elections', London, Constitution Unit April 2000.

8 Private information via Professor Lindsay Paterson, University of Edinburgh.

9 For further detail, see Graham Leicester, 'Scotland', in Hazell, *The State of the Nations*, op. cit.

After Multiculturalism

YASMIN ALIBHAI-BROWN

SEEDS have now been planted, which will, hopefully, lead all Britons to grow into to a new sense of themselves as active participants in a collective enterprise. The Human Rights Act is in place; the idea of dynamic, self conscious individual responsibility and involvement is becoming ever more important; the Lords reforms have implications far beyond constitutional rearrangements; we have started debating the monarchy seriously and class deference is slowly fading away. As Jonathan Freedland, Tom Nairn[1] and other writers have argued, we need to be connected in more meaningful ways than through our existing institutions and emblems which no longer work or resonate as in times gone by. The citizenship culture is upon us and I would like to argue that with the national landscape reshaping itself so dramatically, old multiculturalism—which I offer a detailed critique of in my pamphlet *After Multiculturalism*[2]—has come to the end of its useful life. All societies and communities need to take stock periodically to assess whether existing cultural and political edifices are keeping up with the people and the evolving habitat. Nothing is forever. The most progressive ideas which are right and appropriate at one historical moment can, in time, decay or become defensively self-protective. Old multiculturalism may have reached that point in 21st Century Britain. It does not inspire the young and cannot embrace the most important social developments which are taking place for fear of losing out. It blocks the imagination needed to comprehend and respond to the changes described above. And it is disabling Britons of colour from seeing themselves as key shapers of the emerging citizenship culture. Devolution—an important step, put into place by New Labour—has nevertheless set into motion a process of fragmentation and re-invented nationalisms which may imperil the ideal of an open state with diversity at the heart of it. A Mori survey in the *Economist* in November 1999 revealed that only 18 per cent of Scots, 27 per cent of Welsh identified with Britain. In England the figure rose to 43 per cent, but even here 41 per cent described themselves as English and 49 per cent felt an affinity with their regions above all else. Only 22 per cent of all those interviewed felt confidence in our national parliament at Westminster.[3]

The English will have their own parliament before long. Too many groups, now also including the Scots, Welsh and English, have only a competitive agenda where they struggle against other communities for resources and power and for cultural superiority. They do not really see the world view of others. Where once people of colour were happy to call themselves black, we are now Asian, Hindu, Caribbean, African, Muslim, Shia Muslims, Kashmiris, Khalistanis. This then gives us a platform for making demands which are not

Published by Blackwell Publishers, 108 Cowley Road, Oxford OX4 1JF, UK and 350 Main Street, Malden, MA 02148, USA

only positive, but also negative, against other groups. Liberals who were once happy to be multiculturalists (because it was easy) now have grave reservations about the project, particularly since the crisis over the Salman Rushdie's book, *Satanic Verses*. People of faith across religions are more allied with each other than with secular liberals. It was this alliance which upset New Labour plans to abolish Section 28.[4]

Our national identity is in a state of flux and is causing endless anxieties. It is not only the right wing which is affected. The recent furore over the Parekh Report on the future of multi-ethnic Britain, shows how impossibly difficult this issue has become.[5] The *Daily Telegraph* led the way, the Union Jack flying furiously to denounce all those (including me) who wish to transform the meaning of Britishness. The *Mail* followed as did Jack Straw, who pointed out that an editorial in the *Guardian* had been equally scathing of the idea that Britishness was problematic. This editorial was written by Malcolm Dean, editor of the *Guardian* Society pages, who confirmed that he had written his opinions without reading the report and after reading the *Telegraph*.[6] The *New Statesman*—increasingly eager not to be seen as politically correct—ran a response written by an Indian living in New Delhi, who said he had had a very pleasant time in Oxford once.

The uncertainties produced by globalisation are creating new insecurities across the planet. People in this country seem both to understand how global business enables the making of immeasurable economic gains, but also how this creates a loss of control, of self-determination, cultural annihilation and greater global devastation and inequalities especially as there is no escape from this force. As Andrew Marr put it, 'global power is inside the products that are inside our houses and inside the computer web that is now inside our heads'.[7] In many cases the reaction to this bewildering opening up of our lives has been a greater (and more idealised) identification with old histories and smaller, neater identities.

Although enlightened political leaders are increasingly talking about diversity and our connectedness to Europe and globalised economies, there is much work to be done before a real confidence settles in again. Stuart Hall agrees that this is a testing time for both old fashioned multiculturalism and post enlightenment liberalism, with both sides struggling with the enormous implications of their encounter: He states, 'I think one of the things that multiculturalism has done is to problematise some of the traditional political ideologies leaving unresolved the two major issues of our times—difference and equality.'[8]

The very concept of citizenship has the capacity to transcend these unresolved polarised debates and to start putting into place binding values that we can all agree to live by, even if these lead to some multicultural losses. It may help to push out the boundaries of old multiculturalisms (which are not strong, flexible or exciting enough) and even older and more tired small island nationalisms. Citizenship values have an expansiveness which is indispensable in the modern world. Multiculturalism and anti-

racism were essential during the Thatcher era to fight for cultural entitlements and racial justice, but both had unforeseen consequences which must
now be addressed.

Multicultural Discourse and Integration

We have made remarkable progress since Mr Powell made speeches about
rivers of blood, and this is most evident in assertive, multifarious cities like
London and Manchester. But we do not yet have the optimistic and integrated
society we all hoped for in spite of thirty years of multicultural theology and
practice. For many British citizens it is a self-evident truth that Britain is now
incontrovertibly a multicultural country. For others this statement feels
patently absurd. They argue that the majority of indigenous people have
yet to meet personally a black or Asian Briton. These people live in their white
enclaves, their lives continuing along settled conventions. In demographic
and geographical terms this is an indisputable truth. Two-thirds of the British
still live within five miles of where they were born. Millions of Britons still
love books by authors such as Bill Bryson,[9] about how delightfully eccentric
and unchanged the British are, and listen to the comfortable Radio 4
programme *The Archers* which, in spite of being set in the Midlands, has no
black local characters darkening any doorsteps.

The glitzy, talked up version of multiculturalism although embraced by a
good many Britons,[10] probably means even less to the Pakistanis and
Bangladeshis, officially among the poorest people in Britain today. 80 per
cent of Pakistanis have incomes which are below half the national average.
Gary Younge wrote that 'London's international reputation as a multicultural
haven, bolstered by Blair's oft repeated references to 'multicultural Britain'
sits uneasily with reality.'[11] Linda Colley is similarly sceptical:

'Politicians and pundits shape existing national identities. They rarely by themselves
invent or sustain them. And while it may be valuable to try to identify core national
values, it is in practice difficult to do so in a way that commands broad assent, unless
you descend to uttering platitudes. This is particularly the case in a multinational,
multicultural, infinitely diverse polity like Britain.'

She gives two examples of communities she lives close to—white people—
in rural Norfolk and Bangladeshis in the East End of London—who do not
buy into the idea of a 'fast paced, high octane multicultural Britain.[12] On the
other hand, those who understand and advocate advanced and deeper
multiculturalism, accept that this remains an ideal which is trying to flower
and which will require determined effort to keep alive and spread.[13]

To most people multiculturalism is something that black folk do and is also
entirely located in domestic urban politics and policies. In part this is because
the entire discourse on multiculturalism in this country has been built around
these assumptions, both by black and white Britons. In local areas throughout
the country people have been encouraged by grant giving bodies and local

politicians to promote themselves as particular 'ethnic minorities'. You get money for projects if you can show that as group A you are more 'excluded' than group B. Rarely do we get the encouragement of projects which foster a sense of common purpose or collective citizenry. Multicultural turf wars are everywhere. Different people lay claim to areas, buildings, political and other institutions. More dangerously those who are gullible, furious and ignorant translate these claims into violence. Stephen Lawrence was killed by young white racists who thought Eltham belonged to them. Damilola Taylor, a newly arrived African child, was bullied by black children who thought he was an unwanted outsider.[14] Young Muslims and Sikhs have been in battle on the streets of west London for the last five years.

How can people with such attitudes absorb the meaning of citizenship? And how would they describe their citizenship allegiances? Do they feel a bond and obligations only with other members of their own tribe?

Anti-Racist and Multicultural Policies

Young white people are not what many idealists imagined they would be by this time in our history. In 1997, the European Youth Survey published by MTV found that young white Britons (16–24 year olds) were the most racist in Europe: 30 per cent disagreed that all races and cultures are equal and 26 per cent said they would never date anyone who was of a different colour. Many of these people were born into multiculturalism. In Germany, by contrast, 19 per cent disagreed that all races and cultures were equal.[15] In a powerful and disturbing study carried out in 1996, the academic Roger Hewitt examined the attitudes of young racist thugs in Greenwich, the area where teenagers Stephen Lawrence, Rohit Duggal and Rolan Adams were killed in racist attacks. He found that there is more mature awareness of what it means to live in a multi-ethnic society but that this has made extreme racism worse in certain neighbourhoods. At school in particular, white children have been alienated by the way multiculturalism was played out where all previously colonised societies were uncritically 'celebrated' and white civilisations implicitly accused and undermined. There is essential work to be done on providing a more relevant and inclusive curricula, but you do not redress past injustices by inflicting guilt on or diminishing those who are three generations removed from those who were responsible. But that is what happened in far too many cases. As Hewitt says: 'White pupils, to some extent, seem like cultural ghosts, haunting as mere absences the richly decorated corridors of multicultural societies.'[16]

In an ironic twist, however, some of those who have most resented multiculturalism are now resorting to using the arguments perfected by multiculturalists. A very angry representative of the Countryside Alliance told Andrew Marr that his folk were the new despised minority in this 'multicultural' society.[17] In 1999 the Commission of Racial Equality had a number of complaints from English Britons about discrimination against them by the Scots; and a major investigation into racism in prisons launched in 2000 by the CRE includes a prison in Wales where English prisoners are complaining about discrimination against them.

Ties That Bind

Social democrats have got to find a way of responding which allows for the tribal needs of all Britons and yet can rejuvenate the national spirit; forge a deeper attachment to the European Union and also foster a sense of global connectedness. All this must be underpinned by ideals of human rights and justice. Gordon Brown best describes this when he said: 'As the Tebbit "cricket test" and the Stephen Lawrence case illustrate, there are those who would retreat from an expansive idea of Britishness into a constricted shell of right wing nationalism. My vision of Britain comes not from uniformity but from celebrating diversity, in other words a multi-ethnic and multinational Britain—outward looking, open, internationalist with a commitment to democracy and to tolerance.'[18] Progressive people need to promote the view that this island belongs to everyone and that it is confident enough to progress devolution and feel empowered by the ever changing demographic profiles and cultural inflows which are a condition of modernity. It is only the unimaginative or the uncourageous who fear this. But for the centre to hold, there are binding values based on human rights and social responsibilities which apply to everyone. Those societies which have unacceptably unequal gender roles will have to surrender these for the greater good. Those with an inflated view of their own greatness will have to do the same. No group has more rights than any other. There needs to be a recognition that fundamentalist secular liberalism (based entirely on individual rights and freedoms) diminishes too much the need for individuals to belong and believe. We need social spaces in which we can strive for an integration and a cross-fertilisation of ideas which can be interrogated by others.

This has serious implications. There can be no room for an established religion, nor any state funded denominational schools. Arts funding instead of going largely to 'establishment' art and then 'ethnic art' should foster artists from all backgrounds who are negotiating integration, cultural enlightenment and growth.

All this is best achieved if we become a nation of 'live' citizens. Linda Colley has usefully suggested that we should develop a Millennium Charter for Citizens or a Contract of Citizenship Rights. This is a good starting point. But unlike other such national statements, Britain could create the first ever multi-tiered citizenship charter. We would need to map out the values of citizenship for active participation in local and domestic political and civic life. The next layer would be the role and responsibilities of active European citizenship; and the third would be based on the rights and responsibilities of global citizenship. Finally, there needs to be a stated set of principles of values, aims and objectives for British citizens living in a globalised world.

YASMIN ALIBHAI-BROWN

Stories to connect and liberate

The integrity of this nation state is under severe pressure. The Internet, migration, e-commerce and multinational co-operations may be exciting but they destabalise customary boundaries and props. Britain is particularly susceptible because of the ubiquity of the English language and because all those institutions and ideas which anchored this nation for so long—the monarchy, and the class structure for example—are losing their grip.[19] Will we just muddle through, as an 'asymmetrical state full of different but inchoate allegiances'[20] or will we need something more substantial to re-connect us?

The old British identity is indeed passing away, as Andrew Marr so memorably has said. So what is to take its place? We can attempt valiantly to revive it; we can mark this passing and then concentrate on local identities and Europe. Or we can make a vibrant new Britishness in which diversity is at the heart and not in the toe nails of the body politic. In some ways this has already started. Increasingly Tony Blair, Gordon Brown and even Jack Straw have been speaking about the nation and its multicultural character rather than 'multicultural communities'. It is a pity therefore that these modern ways of describing this cosmopolitan nation are constantly undermined by these same politicians, nervous not to offend middle England and the *Daily Mail*, who talk carelessly about the threat of 'bogus' asylum seekers and immigrants. You cannot be a cosmopolitan nation if the main narratives about your country dwell on threats (mostly imagined from the 'other') You need other narratives, which reveal a different history and which emphasise connections. This regenerative project has already been initiated in the United States by enlightened people. Berkley Professor Ron Takaki in his excellent book, *A Different Mirror* asks: 'Will Americans of diverse races and ethnicities be able to connect themselves to a larger narrative? Whatever happens we can be sure that much of our society's future will be influenced by which 'mirror' we see ourselves.'[21] We need these ties that bind even more since we have no active written constitution, nor flag worshipping tendencies. Here the challenge is to bind and enthuse by fundamentally rethinking notions of heritage, belonging and greatness. As the critic Maya Jaggi has said, cultural heritage is widely seen as an embodiment of the spirit of a nation, part of the cement of a national identity for what is after all an 'imagined community'.[22]

Instead of saying that Britain has become a multicultural country since the war and that we should learn to 'tolerate' difference, people need to take pride in the fact that Britain has always been a country ready to embrace difference throughout history, albeit sometimes through control and acquisition. Thinking the unthinkable is an essential part of leadership. True globalisation should mean the free movement of capital, goods as well as skills and people. *The Economist* has consistently argued for more liberal and rational immigration policies. Europe, with its ageing population and low birth rates, will require the energy of more immigrants. It is important to release the British population from their own panic about hordes of immigrants. Their good life may depend on it. Politicians need to describe immigration positively. Ugandan Asians reluctantly accepted in 1972 have created 30,000 jobs in the Midlands. We need a proper national audit, mapping out the input of immigrants into the key sectors of our national life.[23]

Education

Everyone from Sir Peter Hall to Sir Herman Ouseley believes that New Labour is continuing the legacy of Thatcher and making it even worse when it comes to the education of our children for the future.[24] The narrow precepts of the national curriculum instituted by the 1988 Education Act make little sense today. This legislation was enacted by Margaret Thatcher, whose vision for this country was inward and backward looking, except when it came to libertarian economics. In schools, colleges and universities, black and white children must be taught their connected yet diverse heritage. Equality and only equality can ensure such an exchange. Both will need to go beyond these historical identities, while remaining connected to them. They will also need to develop a deep affinity to Europe and to their diasporic communities while learning ways of critically interrogating both. No black or Asian child should be left to detach herself from Shakespeare and Tolstoy. No white child should be ignorant about C. L. R. James or Salman Rushdie even if they never get round to reading their words. The complex histories of Empire and slavery (including the culpability of non-white people) should be a central part of the history syllabus. This kind of curriculum would foster integration and real dialogue.

Citizenship education is another tool which will prove to be ground-breaking although 'multiculturalists' are concerned that race is not given enough space and is submerged by other more broad based ideas These are misguided concerns. This is the way to avoid the mistakes made by those promoting multicultural education in the late 20th century. It is about all children. The emerging curriculum concentrates on values, participation, respect and an open minded approach to knowledge which for too long has been deliberately restricted by the powerful and (ironically) the power-less.

The curriculum for the future would incorporate cosmopolitanism, 'Euro-peanism', local, ethnic, religious and regional identities. It would teach Muslim children to see themselves as European Muslims and English children to see themselves as European Englanders. They would also be proud to be British, participants in a global economy, as well as in international bodies and conventions and upholders of common human rights.

The same points can be made of the cultural media and sporting sectors

They need to open up to the worlds within the nation as well as the world outside. One remarkable example is the recent news that Andrew Lloyd Webber's next production is based on Bollywood films and will use the considerable talents of an Indian songwriter who writes songs for these films. The show will be staged in London's West End. British Asians will flock to the show and white theatre goers will learn about the biggest film industry in the world. This mutuality is an essential part of the process which will give us the new Britain. We need more such adventurers in the world of the arts and media. Just as American culture and sports have joined the bloodstream of this society, so should all those other world views and experiences. The new Tate gallery is starting to make such a reality, as has the ICA which has transformed itself in the past five years, bringing in people outside the world of white designers as a matter of course and not as a worthy venture, a charitable gesture towards multiculturalism. When the ICA exhibited the work of Steve McQueen, it was the first time ever that a black artist had been given this kind of prominence. And it was not a gift to the gods of multiculturalism or to placate grant givers who like diversity audits these days. Chinese art, Bollywood and African films are as much part of the core activities of the institute which is ambitiously open, critical and cosmopolitan. The Department for Culture, Media and Sport too often ghettoises or excludes non white people. All the top people in the department are white and the department's annual report for 1999 as well as Chris Smith's book, *Creative Britain*[25] barely nods in the direction of cosmopolitanism. Yet Smith, more than most, knows what needs to be done. At an Arts Council conference on heritage he said: 'diversity is a fundamental feature of British culture and it is what makes it, in many ways, rather special. We need to draw all of those rich strands together if we are to come to a proper understanding of what British cultures are about . . . For a society to know that there is more than one interpretation of particular events or periods of history, we must be shown them . . . [there is a] need to provide a more complex version of the truth.'[26]

There needs to be a complete rethink in every sector to do with the arts. Social memory which depends on the stories we tell about ourselves should be re-cast.[27] Vast areas of success, the British Film industry for example, remain stubbornly white. A deliberate decision was made by those making the popular film *Notting Hill*, that no black people would feature and that the Carnival would be left out, even though the story takes place over an entire year. The main output of Radio 4 is similarly small minded and white, except for the odd programmes on racism or multiculturalism. Any public funding of such projects needs to ensure that cultural white heartlands change and modernise and emulate those who have already begun the process. The best example at present is the British Council, which is rapidly moving away from its image of an old Imperial institution to one that is dynamic, modern, diverse and internationally valued.

Politics

A new strategy using the vocabulary of citizenship should be developed in this country. Political leaders should plan this strategy to include attitudes to Europe, diversity within the British Isles and globalisation. Joined up government means that the Foreign Office, Home Office, the Department of Trade and Industry, the Department of Overseas Development, Cabinet Office, the Department of Education and Employment, the Department of Culture, Media and Sport can now work together and begin a process of change. We can learn from other countries. In Canada diversity is encouraged within strong boundaries of commonality. The project is steered by the federal government and the central principles of equality, diversity and common values are reinforced by policies, speeches and citizenship rights. The word includes indigenous people, the English and the French and all other immigrants groups. Like the new South Africa, in spite of some resistance, the country proudly defines itself positively as a nation of various peoples.[28] Both countries have extended international responsibilities and take pride in this fact. The always threatening isolationism of the United States is rarely, if ever, seen in Canada.

The only logical institutional framework to facilitate the changes described above is a Human Rights Commission. All citizens must be enabled to get redress if they are discriminated against. They include the young, the old, white, Asian, black and other Britons, gay people, women, lone parents, those locked in poverty, people who follow various religions and so on. To have only some of these people protected, while others suffer injustices is not only unfair, but extremely unwise: it makes the unprotected victims resent the laws and institutions which exist to help particular groups.

A vibrant common citizenship culture which can foster genuine respect, equality and consideration across various groups and diversity, together with tough anti-discrimination measures may just give us the kind of country that so many of us yearn for. The challenge is for us to persuade those who are determined to go back to the future, the cynics who see such ideas as vacuous and sentimental; and those who still feel wedded purely to multicultural solutions.

Notes

1 J Freedland, *Bring Home the Revolution*, London, Fourth Estate, 1998; and T. Nairn, *After Britain*, London, Granta, 2000.
2 Published by the Foreign Policy Centre, 2000.
3 November 1999.
4 Iqbal Sacramie of the Muslim Council of Britain presented this idea on *National Portrait*, Analysis, BBC, Radio 4, 2 Nov. 1999.
5 The Parekh Report, Runnymede Trust, published by Profile, 2000.
6 See Stuart Hall's letter in the *Guardian*, 15 Nov. 2000.

7 *The Day Britain Died*, Profile, 2000, p. 134. This book accompanied the television series with the same title referred to below.

8 Interview with the author for *National Portrait*, op. cit.

9 In *Notes from a Small Island*, Bill Bryson says he loves, 'Marmite, village fetes, country lanes, haymaking in June, stinging nettles, seaside piers, Ordnance survey maps, crumpets, hot water bottles.'

10 For a good example of this view, see Mark Leonard, *Britain TM: Renewing our identity*, London, Demos, 1997.

11 *Evening Standard Magazine*, 25 Feb. 2000.

12 Downing Street Millennium Lecture, *Britishness in the 21st century*, January 2000.

13 Professor Stuart Hall acknowledged this on Radio 4, *Desert Island Discs*, 13 Feb. 2000.

14 See my column, *The Independent*, 2 Dec. 2000.

15 Report published in February 1997.

16 Roger Hewitt, *The Roots of Racism, The Social Basis of Racist Action*, London, Trentham Books, p. 40.

17 BBC2, *The Day Britain Died*, 2 Feb, 2000.

18 *Guardian*, 12 Nov. 1998.

19 See Chapter 1 of Yasmin Alibhai-Brown, *Who Do We Think We Are?*, Harmondsworth, Penguin, 2000.

20 Linda Colley, 'Britishness in the 21st Century': Downing St Millennium Lectures, 8 Dec. 1999, p. 8. (See www.number-10.gov.uk for full text.

21 Little, Brown, 1993, p. 17.

22 *Guardian*, 3 Nov. 1999.

23 ibid.

24 Chris Smith, *Creative Britain*, London, Faber, 1998.

25 *Whose Heritage?*, op. cit. . . . (where?)

26 For details, see Yasmin Alibhai-Brown, *True Colours*, London, IPPR, 1999.

27 See my pamphlet, *After Multiculturalism*, op. cit.

28 For details, see *True Colours*, London, IPPR, 2000.

How European Can We/Will We Be?

NEAL ASCHERSON

To reach any answers, some assumptions have to be made about this question. And the first assumption is that 'we' can be interpreted in several ways, leading to several divergent conclusions. 'We' may denote the inhabitants of Britain, or of the United Kingdom. On the other hand, it could stand for the English, the Scots, the Welsh, the people of Northern Ireland and the populations of the various autonomous small islands in the archipelago—taken severally, or taken in various combinations. (For example, it might make a sort of sense to compose two prospects of 'Europeanness': an English prospect, and another for all the other UK and archipelago components lumped together.)

However we take that, it is also true that no question about the future ('can we/will we?') can be tackled before it has been asked about the present ('are we/do we?'). And here some generalisations do seem to emerge. There is nothing strikingly non-European about Scotland. There is much about Wales, from its linguistic politics to its trade patterns in recent history, which resembles the experience of many small European nations (Sweden, Latvia, the Basque country etc.). Northern Ireland, in political-science terms the lair of 17th century coelocanths, finds no parallel or indeed comprehension in 21st century Europe. But England as a nation is a much trickier question. If the nation and its 'everyday' culture can be distinguished from its institutions and political culture, then English daily life and daily attitudes are (language excepted) closer to those of the Germans or the Dutch than to those of the citizens of Massachusetts or Texas. When it comes to sinking a bore-hole into 'Britain', on the other hand, the elements found in the core taken from this state structure and its institutional culture are sharply unlike a geological core from contemporary European polities; but equally unlike any sampling of United States political culture. Put very coarsely and provocatively, Scotland and Wales (and conceivably, but not convincingly, England) may be European nations, but 'Britain' certainly is not.

Britain as an early-modern state, the outcome of a long process of English expansion, was organised (as Linda Colley has so often suggested) around three main and related principles: the securing of an anti-Catholic state under a Protestant succession; the preservation of that Protestant dynasty by war and alliance against continental rivals; and the maintenance and defence of a trans-oceanic empire. All three principles implied a defensive *Abgrenzung*: a fencing-off from the main body of Europe, and a turning-away of preoccupation from the further shore of the Channel towards, first, the Atlantic and all that lay beyond it and, secondly, introvertedly, towards Britain itself.

NEAL ASCHERSON

Ideas of Europe

The second prior definition required is what we mean by 'European'. Timothy Garton Ash, lecturing at the Royal Institute of International Affairs in November 2000, selected five ironic but widespread versions of what being 'European' can signify. They were

(1) to be perceived as 'white';
(2) to be geographically associated with Europe;
(3) to be a member-state of the European Union;
(4) to be not just a member but a fully-participating, paid-up enthusiast for 'the European Project'; and
(5) to observe supposedly 'European' values and standards of behaviour (as in: 'The politics of Hitler or Haider are not "European"').

For the purposes of discussing relative qualities of citizenship, only the last one is useful. But I would narrow its focus a little. The European standard which is relevant is what can be loosely called 'republican principle'. In other words, most European states (in or out of the EU, with or without mon-archies) subscribe to a particular bundle of constitutional standards which originate in the Enlightenment. These are:

(1) the theory of popular sovereignty;
(2) the related notion that power flows upwards from the base of the social pyramid to the apex;
(3) the doctrine of a supreme law—usually embodied in a Constitution— which is the ultimate authority in the state and to which all elected bodies and all officials of the Executive are subject;
(4) the idea of individual human rights, specific and justiciable, which the state exists to protect.

It will be seen that none of the first three standards are applicable to the British state system. Sovereignty resides in the Crown-in-Parliament (i.e. in the House of Commons) under a doctrine of parliamentary absolutism. The Crown (i.e. in practice the Cabinet and the Executive) is the fount of power, which is distributed downwards at the discretion of sovereign authority and is revocable at any time. No codified supreme law or constitution exists, and if it did, it would not bind Parliament which would remain entitled to disregard or even revoke it at pleasure.

However, the fourth standard—the doctrine of human rights—has now powerfully and irrevocably entered British awareness. It was introduced initially from the United States rather than from Europe (the main import dating back to the Presidency of Jimmy Carter in the 1970s, and to his insistence on inserting a doctrine of universal human rights into the East/West dialogue of the Cold War). Although it is not logically compatible with English/British traditions of authority and sovereignty, the doctrine has now been embodied in domestic Scottish and English legislation (after many years in which British subjects were obliged to litigate for their rights before the European Commission and Court of Human Rights).

Critics of the British system (Charter 88, for example) used to complain that the British were 'subjects', but not 'citizens'. By this they meant (among other things) that a British subject had in the strict sense no civil rights. This is less true today than it was ten years ago. Although the British doctrine of state persists without formal amendment, the 'rights culture' is now firmly embedded in popular and political consciousness. It is a change which has its positive sides (the arrival of a Human Rights Act, for example) and its unlovely aspects, like the wildfire spread of litigation in pursuit of compensation for real or imagined breach of rights. What matters is that it is apparently irreversible, and that this change brings the British subject measurably nearer to the status of the European citizen. Another change which has taken place, also tending to entrench the subject's capacity to resist the state, is the rapid growth of judicial review hearings in the courts. The judiciary may find that the executive has acted unlawfully, or contrary to any reasonable interpretation of an Act or regulation. In effect, the executive here consents to a derogation of parliamentary absolutism by allowing itself to be overruled by a judge in a court of law. This is not the same as introducing a full code of 'administrative law', on the Continental model. Still less does it amount to any gradual assembling of a do-it-yourself constitution. All the same, as the years pass, a sort of fabric of administrative-law precedent is beginning to build up. Here again, British practice in matters affecting the exercise of citizenship is beginning to come closer to European norms.

The British Sonderweg

Closer—but not yet close. There can be no disputing the fact that England/Britain has until now followed a *Sonderweg*—an exceptional track of historical development. Historians argue vividly about when this divergence from the main European path took place; Norman Davies in his *The Isles: A History* (Macmillan 1999) (the first major study of the British past to escape the anglocentric hall of mirrors in which almost all other histories have been composed) is certain that the departure took place at the Henrician Reformation. Others, for example Richard Hodges in his *The Anglo-Saxon Achievement* (Duckworth 1989), believes that England left Europe far earlier, when a Saxon class of competitive, entrepreneurial peasants established its palaeo-Thatcherite credentials. The question is whether the Anglo-British state of today can now converge further with European practices of citizenship, or whether convergence has already gone as far as it can without collapsing the whole Britannic edifice.

There are in a sense two categories of EU member-nation, or aspirant to membership. One is pragmatic, but the other is apocalyptic. The pragmatic members, like France and the Benelux countries back in the earliest years of the Rome Treaty, joined up for concrete and achievable goals which were not in themselves controversial at home: the prevention of European war, the prosperity to be gained from customs union and industrial co-ordination. The apocalyptic members, in contrast, joined in order to settle, once and for all, enormous arguments about national destiny which divided their countries. Chancellor Adenauer, for instance, committed West Germany to the West, locking the door on the option of a united, semi-socialist, neutral Germany between the Cold War blocs. The leaders of Ireland today, by opting for Europe and Celtic tigerhood in a free market, are hoping that the golden torrents of the EU will wash away what remains of the older national vision: an austere, pious island meditating on its own faded flags, uncontaminated by foreign materialism. A third example: liberal and modernising Poles believe that by invoking the Union they are pre-empting the insoluble argument between Catholic-nationalist isolationism and an outward-looking Poland which would reform its public life along western European lines.

There are some apocalyptic Europeans even in England. Those who believe British democracy to be decrepit would throw open the sluices and let in Europe to drown all the courtiers and Druids and fish-footmen who still insist that British institutions are 'the best in the world'. But such desperate spirits are few. There are plenty of people in England who believe that the EU has posed 'an enormous argument about national destiny'. But for them, the argument is between sovereignty and super-state, between the two equally imaginary extremes of an island kingdom unhampered by any external restraints and a 'federal' Europe as monolithic as Imperial Rome or the Third Reich. These are cartoon horror fantasies; they can only summon Europe to annihilate Britain, never to reform it.

Meanwhile the old British attitude to citizenship is tenacious, not least because it is endearing and satisfying. As Ann Dummett has written, the very word has warm, unpolitical associations: 'For many people in Britain, citizenship means involvement with the community: good citizenship requires honesty, reliability, helping one's neighbour and working voluntarily for good causes. It is a social norm for all residents: nobody thinks it odd that foreigners should have recourse to a Citizens' Advice Bureau or be called "good citizens" for their local activities.'[1] Dummett observes that British notions of citizenship have little to do with nationality, whereas French or German definitions are far more political—and exclusive. 'A French citizen is supposed to be guaranteed individual freedom, civic rights and duties, cultural identity and membership of a nation . . . In Germany, the sense of ethnic Germanness is combined with attachment to language and culture and a sharply defined set of rights which foreigners cannot share.'

There is something appealing in this colloquial good-citizenship, which carries with it membership of civil society but not formal membership of the political nation—no 'civis brittanicus sum'. The reverse side of the coin, though, is subjecthood: a membership of the kingdom, feudally defined, which carries duties but only a haphazard bundle of rights. 'By the time of the Second World War, a subject had the right to vote and stand for office in the United

Kingdom, work in the public service, serve in the armed forces and be master of a British ship' (ibid.).

Indescribable Muddle

Today the British legislation covering citizenship, nationality and subjecthood is an indescribable muddle. The best that can be said is that it is a muddle in motion, as the habit of appealing to the innate or intrinsic rights of the individual floods irreversibly across the British Isles. People increasingly speak and act as if they were citizens, although formally they are not. The old recourse of 'I'll take it to my MP' has been overshadowed by the threat of legal action, whether through the European Court of Human Rights, through the new Human Rights Act or through judicial review of an executive decision. This is clearly a shift towards a European view of citizenship, the fully-accredited club member calling on the staff to do the jobs he pays them for. Must it mean shifting away from that informal 'good citizenship' based on mutual support rather than contract? I cannot see why it should, any more than why a thriving political society should grow at the expense of civil society. Both are compatible. But the coming of the rights culture does, inevitably, bring with it something else which is distinctly European: a more positive view of lawyers.

The republican nations which grew out of the Enlightenment, with their codified and constitutional structures, set lawyers high. The existence of administrative law ensured that, in most Continental countries, a law degree is still the essential qualification for a civil service or political career. In contrast to Britain, lawyers are not associated exclusively with set-piece murder or libel trials, but are also perceived as the thin black line defending the citizen from the state's abuse of power. Judges are much younger, because the judging career is usually separate (the British assumption that the bench is crammed with senile reactionaries unable to carry on at the Bar is not a 'European' point of view). And open political commitment among Continental, Roman-law advocates is much more common than in England (it has long been the custom in Scotland). Why not? After all, *lex rex*—the constitution is the supreme law above all legislatures.

Admittedly, this new respect for lawyers will take some time to develop, especially in England. The tradition that lawyers are greedy, lazy and arrogant will die hard. And the tradition that lawyers should at all costs be kept away from 'political' decision-making—a favourite with old-fashioned zealots for the privileges of Parliament—will be long-lived too. And yet the rights culture must lead to a sweeping political enfranchisement of lawyers. It is they, after all, who must operate that culture in ways that satisfy mass demand, and it is already true that somewhere, every week of the year, an elected Cabinet minister is being informed by barristers and judges that he or she has misinterpreted a statute and must back down.

It can be accepted that European norms about codified rights, the legal accountability of government, the fairness of certain electoral systems and so on will continue to seep into Anglo-British practice. The question here is whether quantity will ultimately become quality. It seems likely that the day will come when the sheer weight of imported innovations based on doctrines of popular sovereignty finally brings down the roof of Westminster Hall and buries the whole authoritarian tradition of parliamentary sovereignty under its ruins. But there is much more to citizenship than political rights. There are other freedoms and opportunities which pertain to a 'participative' citizenship and which are obtainable across the Channel. The most striking group are to do with work: with the 'social partnership' concept of a common project between capital and labour which is a widespread, even venerable plank of the Christian Democrat and Social Democrat worldview.

Here there are few encouraging answers to 'how European can we be'. Neither, on this point, are there significant differences between the component nations of the British state. There is an all-British tradition of private management, and a hard-fisted, autocratic, Victorian tradition it remains. 'Social partnership' has until recently been regarded with almost equal contempt by capital and labour in Britain. For the employer, state measures to regulate factory conditions and wages have merely represented interference, sometimes unavoidable, with the sovereign rights of the entrepreneur to handle his investment as he pleases. The employee is a subject in his place of work, whatever rights he or she may enjoy outside. The thought that active participation in management and planning by the workforce could actually increase profitability is rarely encountered in Britain. So great was the bellow of disbelieving horror which went up in 1991, when it seemed that Maastricht might introduce a mild form of worker-participation into British boardrooms, that the United Kingdom opted out of the whole 'Social Chapter'.

It is difficult to speak of 'economic citizenship' in a climate which regards— for instance—German *Mitbestimmung* as tantamount to Bolshevism. But this is a situation where the gulf between British and European attitudes has actually grown wider. The return to Victorian economic liberalism after 1979 did not merely castrate trade union power and sweep away much of Britain's traditional industrial base. It ushered in a much more 'American' structure of free-market capitalism, in which investment in the future of an enterprise was subordinated to short-term obsession with the stock price and the shareholders. The losers in this process were invariably the employees, subjected to wave after wave of 'de-layering' and redundancy. Meanwhile an American management culture was introduced to de-skill and atomise labour forces, in order to prevent the claiming or exercise of employee rights.

Worse than the archaism of Britain's institutions, this autocracy in the workplace is the tallest barrier across the way to a more participative citizenship. And it shows few signs of weakening. In December 2000, news that the European Union was drafting an agreement to regulate and discourage hostile take-over bids was greeted with sheer incredulity in London. When Brussels suggested that regulation would protect the jobs and rights of employees, who were entitled to be consulted about the fate of their firm, a London stock exchange spokeswoman merely replied that uncontrolled competition would in the end lead to more job creation. It is between London and Brussels, not in some Islamic continent, that Professor Samuel Huntington's 'civilizational clash' is taking place.

Note

1 Ann Dummett, in Robert Hazell, ed., *Constitutional Futures; a History of the Next Ten Years*, Oxford, OUP, 1999.

Culture and Citizenship

ANTHONY EVERITT

IN what sense can it be argued that the arts help to promote active or participative citizenship? In large part, the answer lies in history and in the need to correct its distortions. The founding chairman of the Arts Council of Great Britain (ACGB), John Maynard Keynes, would have been puzzled by the question and might very well not have deigned to respond. He was suspicious of the Arts Council's wartime predecessor, the Council for the Encouragement of Music and the Arts (CEMA), one of whose objectives was the 'promotion of music-making and play-acting by the people themselves'. When planning the new Council, which came into being in 1945, Keynes wrote: 'I was worried lest what one may call the welfare side was to be developed at the expense of the artistic side, and standards generally.' As it found its feet in the years following the Second World War, the new body followed Keynes's lead, seeing art as a good in itself, to which only the better off and the better educated had access. Like money, it needed to be redistributed to all citizens.

There was, however, another long-established tradition of creative parti- cipation, represented by CEMA and stretching back into the 19th century. It included choral singing, brass bands, amateur theatre, the folk revival and more recently aspects of jazz and rock. The Arts Council (and its successors, the Arts Council of England, the Scottish Arts Council, the Arts Council of Wales, together with the Arts Council of Northern Ireland) showed little interest in these cultural manifestations and, although they touched many people's lives, undervalued them. They regarded their dual task as being to promote aesthetic excellence and raise attendances. So they concentrated their attention on creating a subsidised national network of professional (mainly performing) arts institutions.

The Arts Councils have been successful in realising much of what they set out to do. Production has greatly expanded and standards are high. Geo- graphical access has been widened and audiences have risen. However, these achievements have been offset by a crucial failure: while increasing the number of attenders, the Arts Councils have not significantly extended their social reach. This has come to the attention of government, which has begun to recognise the potential social impacts of the arts, the growing economic importance of intellectual property in a global economy driven by the new information technologies and the consequential need to stimulate creativity among its citizens.

As a result, the present UK Government and its predecessor have sought to move from arts policy to cultural policy: that is, to enlarge the state's concern, expressed through the arm's-length funding system, for the arts as tradition-

© The Political Quarterly Publishing Co. Ltd. 2001
Published by Blackwell Publishers, 108 Cowley Road, Oxford OX4 1JF, UK and 350 Main Street, Malden, MA 02148, USA

ally defined (the so-called 'high' or, in Raymond Williams's phrase, the 'old' arts) to an idea of culture which also embraces participatory practice and mass popular culture in all their forms. This broader definition solves at a stroke the problem of social reach, because it encompasses the interests of the many rather than the few. It also moves the focus of public policy from seeking to remedy a perceived lack of access to culture to enabling everyone to express his or her own culture.

This development offers a clear opportunity to align cultural policy with the promotion of active citizenship. However, to realise this aim is not so straightforward as might appear. There are two ways in which we may understand a citizenship culture. First, it can denote the participation of citizens in governance, whether it be by entering active politics, voting in elections or demonstrating practical concern about the social and economic issues about which government takes decisions. According to this view, to cite Aristotle, the man or woman who is not *politicos*, who does not take part in politics, does not deserve to be a *politēs*, a citizen.

In the 20th century, some modern states put the arts to this purpose. The former Soviet Union and Nazi Germany saw them as a useful means of forming active citizens by promoting commitment to a ruling ideology and a powerful concept of national identity. Thus Bertolt Brecht's *lehrstücke*, such as his play, *The Measures Taken*, were straightforwardly didactic and attempted to persuade the audience to adopt the behaviour of an ideal Communist Party member.

The Post-War Scene

During the period of reconstruction after the Second World War, a similar objective (among others) motivated some European democracies to invest in the arts—with the crucial distinction that they wished to win support, not for a regime, but for the nation state itself. Two examples illustrate the point. Finland's commitment to culture, and especially music, represented a conscious attempt to recreate an integrated and self-confident society. French cultural policy since de Gaulle has followed the example of Louis XIV and devoted substantial resources to the pursuit of *la gloire*. The development in the United Kingdom of Arts Councils at arm's length from government might suggest that politicians here took a more disinterested approach, merely supposing that it was the mark of a civilised society to possess a thriving cultural scene. However, it may be no accident that by far the largest part of the Arts Council's subsidies is awarded to prestige institutions which celebrate the British and more broadly the European heritage in which it is imbedded. The cult of Shakespeare has not only marked a recognition of his greatness, but reflects his contribution to a certain idea of Britain, which has, as a consequence, been of value to the tourist industry and the cultural diplomacy of the British Council.

In this connection it is interesting to note the weight placed on the identity-forming function of culture by the newly devolved governments in Scotland and Wales. A key aim of the Scottish national cultural strategy is *Creating Our Future, Minding Our Past* is to 'increase opportunities for celebrating Scotland's culture both in Scotland and abroad'. In Wales a debate is proceeding (at the time of writing) as to whether the National Assembly should promote the arts in Wales or Welsh arts. At the local level many large cities, such as Glasgow and Birmingham, have made culture a leading priority as part of a strategy of 'city imaging'.

However, if cultural policy in the United Kingdom is at least partly designed to stimulate a notion of nationhood, civic celebration and perhaps civic loyalty, few political leaders would go so far as to claim that the arts encourage in any direct way active citizenship. For such a view we must look elsewhere in a different and surprising quarter. In the 1960s the partly submerged tradition of creative participation took a new turn with the emergence of the community arts movement. Its original proposition was that arts had been appropriated by the ruling classes and were a means of bolstering their authority. A leading community artist of the day, Su Braden, wrote: 'It is only through actively engaging with society that artists may acquire a perception of reality which matches that of ordinary people in local contexts.'[1] Her aim and that of many others in the field was to recognise that everyone owned her or his culture, but was debarred from expressing it. The task of a community artist was to place her or his skills at the disposal of people in disadvantaged neighbourhoods so that they could develop their cultural awareness. This reflected less an acknowledgement of the intrinsic value of art than a belief that engagement with artistic creation would empower people to speak up for themselves in the public arena and resist the perceived oppression of government policies and the state's bureaucratic apparatus. In the ensuing decades community arts practice spread and to some degree lost its original political edge. Today almost every large theatre, dance or opera company and orchestra have established education and community outreach departments, which offer a diet of community-based arts programmes, but usually without the underpinning of socialist ideology.

So to recapitulate, public subsidy of the arts in the United Kingdom has not directly promoted active or participatory citizenship in its political definition. However, the example of community arts is moderating this view and the cultural sector has adopted a commitment, of varying degrees of seriousness, to community development and individual empowerment.

A Vigorous Civil Society

There is a second kind of active citizenship where a participatory approach to artistic practice has real significance: namely, the promotion of a vigorous civil society. According to Salvador Giner, 'civil society is an historically evolved sphere of individual rights, freedoms and voluntary associations whose politically undisturbed competition with each other in the pursuit of their respective private concerns, interests, preferences and intentions is guaranteed by a public institution, called the state.'[2]

Civil citizenship in this sense does not express itself through involvement in the operations of the state, in public life, but in a zone where the state has no role except to guarantee its frontiers. This is the world of arts clubs, photography societies, *Eisteddfoddau*, Gilbert and Sullivan companies, the Friends of the Royal Opera House and much else besides. More than 100,000 people are members of a range of amateur arts 'umbrella' organisations (such as the British Federation of Young Choirs and the Embroiderers' Guild). This figure only hints at the full extent of participation in creative activity. According to the Arts Council of Great Britain *RSGB Omnibus Arts Survey* of 1991[3] two per cent of the adult population claim to participate in amateur music/drama, eleven per cent in textile crafts, eight per cent in painting and drawing and five in playing a musical instrument. When all forms of creative activity are taken into account millions of Britons join clubs and associations to practise an art or a craft.

These myriad arts activists are a vital component of a lively civil society where, with benevolent selfishness, citizens, singly or in groups, cultivate their special interests. They do so from choice and usually have as little as possible to do with the public sector. As a study of general club culture argues: 'Involvement in such groups offers people something probably unique in our society: the chance to come together with others to create or participate for collective benefit and enjoyment rather than for sale to an anonymous audience or purchaser. This is why their continued existence is important and why these groups are so keen to assert their independence.'[4]

Facilities, venues and small grants are sometimes provided for arts groups of this kind by local councils. Now, with the arrival of National Lottery funding the UK Arts Councils and the English Regional Arts Boards have also begun to intervene. Large sums of money have been finding their way to the amateur and community-based cultural sector. On the one hand, this shift in public arts policy is a welcome recognition that the Arts Councils' traditional Keynesian focus on the interests of the professional artist is widening to include creative activity (in the CEMA phrase) 'by the people themselves.' On the other hand, it means that the frontiers of the state are encroaching on what until now has been a free province of civil society. It is reasonable to fear that the amateur and participatory arts could become a part of public provision and that their voluntary character would be compromised. This would inevitably reduce their value as building blocks of civil citizenship.

The Hand of the State

A glance at the post-War development of professional arts organisations illuminates the nature of the threat. Arts Councils and the English Regional Arts Boards have established development strategies at the behest of government with a view to delivering not only their own, but also governmental priorities. This they cannot do by themselves, because they pass on most of their money to others, so they are obliged to ensure that those they subsidise act on their behalf. Through client funding agreements, arts organisations are obliged to work not only for themselves, but for the government and its agencies This trend can be illustrated by the Culture and Recreation Bill, announced in the Queen's Speech towards the end of 2000, which, if enacted, will require leading museums and galleries to consult the Secretary of State for Culture, Media and Sport before appointing the chairmen of their boards of management. This will give him, in effect, control over these appointments; for which cultural institution would be likely to go against the expressed wishes of its paymaster? At present, while trustees are often appointed by the minister, they often elect their chairmen themselves, thus in practice retaining a significant degree of independence from the government. The measure is a further small, but definite step to transforming these committees from gatherings of private citizens who share a common passion *into state-approved functionaries*. The announced replacement of the RABs by regional offices of the Arts Council of England seems likely to prove a further example of centralisation.

Cultural institutions, then, are becoming as much part of the public sector as a national health service or a police force. However, it would be wrong to overstate the implications of this, for subsidy seldom exceeds 50 per cent of the turnover of performing arts organisations, which are expected to make up the difference by attracting substantial revenue from audiences and devoting energy to winning private sector sponsorship and patronage. Also, there is little evidence that artistic content has been directly constrained or controlled. Nevertheless, the outcome is that performing arts companies now present their work in an official or quasi-official context. If freedom is exercised by permission, the purposes to which that freedom is put may lose something of their force. At the very least, the process of aesthetic creation and presentation no longer emerges as evidently as it once did from the self-interested coming together of private citizens as artists and audiences. Rather, it is produced in and for the public interest. However well-intentioned, government subsidy is a Greek gift.

If it is accepted that the arts, whether professional or participatory, foster active citizenship in the sense that they help to promote a thriving civil society, the government needs to consider how it can act to support them without smothering them. Three courses of action suggest themselves. The first is to make the most of what cannot be easily changed. The government's settled view is that the arts are a weapon in their armoury to be deployed against social exclusion and for cultural diversity and social cohesion. It believes that subsidised orchestras, theatre companies and art galleries, which, as we have seen, have built up substantial experience in the fields of education and community development, have a role to play in this respect.

But if further encroachment by the state into the arts is to be avoided and, even, reversed, the trick will be to provide subsidy where it is necessary to keep cultural institutions in business while at the same time withdrawing so far as possible from direct engagement in their operations. This could be achieved by targeting public resources explicitly on arts programmes which contribute to larger social and economic objectives and pull back from financing core activity—that is, concerts in the concert hall, plays on the stage and exhibitions in the gallery. It would not be practical to advocate a complete retreat from contributing to central running costs, but it should be made clear that grants are primarily offered to enable arts organisations to engage in educational and community-based work. In other words, the purpose of subsidy should be defined no longer as primarily to maintain an on-going arts economy dedicated to professional performance or exhibition, but to buy specific services that are relevant to government's strategic aims.

A Lighter Touch Regime

The present emphasis on the detailed evaluation of everything that arts organisations do, almost as if they were government executive agencies, should be replaced by a lighter regulatory touch, the main aim of which, apart from monitoring general financial probity, would be directed to assessing the effectiveness with which these commissioned services were delivered. This would give them greater responsibility than at present for managing their core activity. There would be risks here, especially in the performing arts, which depend on box-office income to a greater extent than museums, libraries and archives, and so are more prone to financial crisis or even collapse; but the countervailing advantage would be that the cultural sector would gain greater mastery over its own destiny. It would often be in partnership with the state, but not altogether under its own control.

Research will need to be conducted to confirm and refine the social and economic impacts of arts provision more convincingly than is the case at present. Government social programmes, such as the ambitious Targeting Social Need scheme in Northern Ireland, which requires all non-departmental public bodies to support priorities aimed at communities and social groupings at maximum disadvantage, can be unhelpfully blunt instruments when applied to cultural activity. The arts are not a social service, they can do little to improve housing, they do not create many unskilled jobs and are ill-equipped to address long-term unemployment. However, as community artists have long shown, the creative experience *can* help people to develop the confidence to express and to assert themselves—in brief, to associate as active citizens in civil society.

However, if this is the correct and appropriate way of using the arts to address social questions, it is essential that public intervention be project-oriented. The aim must be to create the circumstances which enable citizens to establish free-standing arts groups or projects, brought into being by community-based programmes, but not permanently dependent on them. In other words, the state should act to enlarge or repair civil society and active citizenship, not to replace it. Community Music London, one of the country's most successful participatory projects, offers an example of good practice. The organisation has shown how a carefully co-ordinated programme of training trainers can transform music provision in an area and stimulate the setting up of autonomous music groups. During the 1990s the organisation ran a summer playscheme in the London Borough of Newham with 25 low achievers and school refusers. Two local youth workers were trained in fund-raising and two musicians in managing a music workshop. A number of young people, mainly beginners, formed their own music group. Some went on to study music at college, create further bands or get jobs in the arts. In another project in Newham, Community Music gave music workshops for a group of young Asian people, which in due course became the nationally known Asian Dub Foundation, which has played a major role in bringing Asian musics into the rock and pop mainstream.

The second course of action derives from the growing power of the new information technologies. The world's museums, libraries and archives are digitising their collections and this is transforming their relationship with citizens. IT's key feature is that it is a two-way, not a one-way medium. Once the creator and the curator were like actors on a stage playing to a passive audience sitting in the dark. But now they are becoming partners with the public in a joint enterprise and the conventional distinctions between professional and amateur, between artist and audience are blurring. IT users are no longer simply consumers but producers of culture.

Previously, the marketing and distribution of cultural products—in music and literature for example—were in the hands of publishers of various kinds. The relationships between producers, distributors and consumers are now changing. It is increasingly easy and affordable for individuals at home to do without the middleman and publish their own literary works on the Internet—potentially reaching far wider audiences than traditional print. With the right equipment, they can download, remix and immediately redistribute music, and visual images. We can repeat Marshall McLuhan's joky comment of a quarter of a century ago, but this time as a statement of fact: 'We can all be artists now.'

Virtual museums, libraries and archives put collections within the reach of those who are otherwise denied entry: for geographical or economic reasons, for example. But a good virtual museum is more than a digital slide show. Multimedia systems make available images of, and information about, individual works of art and cultural traditions. More significantly, they allow non-linear forms of inquiry and investigation by users. Through networks and hyperlinks, visitors can make connections between separate collections in many different institutions throughout the world. They can search by theme, artist, date, period or cultural traditions and in many other ways. They can explore links between objects and other items—documents, books, and artefacts—wherever they are physically housed and, in some cases (e.g. the Louvre Museum education website), make their own commentaries or inputs. The networking of resources that virtual museums make possible can enrich understanding of our common heritage by placing them in many different contexts and relationships.

A remarkable initiative illustrates this new interaction between citizen and cultural provider. In Germany the broadcasting company, ARD, has created a website, called Zeitenwende (Changing Times), which allows people to input digitised evidence of their personal participation in historical events of their time. As the Canadian commentator on the impact of IT on culture, Derrick de Kerckhove remarked: 'This is collective memory in action, navigable for totally personal itineraries . . . The addition of raw data, from unexpected sources, does not invalidate the recognised dogmas or the ascertained masterpieces, but it adds to them the evidence of that unconscious part of culture, the life of ordinary people.'[5]

The third, and perhaps the most important, measure which will bring culture into the service of active citizenship, concerns education and addresses economic as well as social objectives. The British public education system since its inception has tended to define intelligence as academic ability, an emphasis that has only been sharpened by the Blair Government's recent prioritisation of numeracy and literacy in schools. Creativity, whether in the arts or other fields of endeavour, has been given comparatively less room in the curriculum. The landmark report, *All Our Futures: Creativity, Culture and Education*, defined creativity in the following terms: 'Our starting point is to recognise four characteristics of creative processes. First, they always involve thinking or behaving *imaginatively*. Second, overall this imaginative activity is *purposeful*: that is, it is directed towards achieving an objective. Third, these processes must generate something *original*. Fourth, the outcome must be of *value* in relation to the objective. We therefore define creativity as: imaginative activity fashioned so as to produce outcomes that are both original and of value.'[6]

Creative skills are in ever greater demand at a time when the nature of the workplace is undergoing rapid and unceasing transformation, and manufacturing has increasingly given place to the creative industries and the provision of services. The new information technologies have brought into being a highly competitive market in the production of intellectual property. Technical, economic and financial change is progressing at such a pace that education based on the acquisition of particular kinds of knowledge and vocational training dedicated to particular skills soon becomes outdated during the passage of a career. Rather, what is likely to be required of workers in future will be the ability to adapt creatively to the changing demands of a global economy.

It follows that a redress of the imbalance in favour of academic studies is urgently required. Greater space for creativity in the curriculum will equip the workers of tomorrow to react constructively to change and so enable the British economy to retain its competitiveness in coming years. What needs to be taught is not only established knowledge, but an open and enquiring aptitude for acquiring new forms of knowledge as they replace the old; also a talent for lateral thinking as problems and challenges present themselves in new and surprising forms.

The arts can make a valuable contribution in this respect. However, they also have another function. Just as the traditional verities of the world of work are disappearing, so social and cultural values are being challenged. It is no longer easy to assert or to maintain absolute standards; and tomorrow's citizens will need to be able to test and develop their own cultural assumptions in an age when migration, travel and modern communications confront them with those of other societies, when the decline of religious belief compels them to shape their own morality without resort to established authority and when traditional, geographically based communities are yielding to a pervasive individualism and to the emergence of provisional communities of shared interests.

The arts offer a unique means of recognising, testing, exploring, subverting and celebrating cultural assumptions. The creative skills required for the workplace are much the same as those by which today we have to live our lives—above all, an ability to respond sensitively to a social environment with fewer fixed reference points than in the past.

In summary, the arts, broadly defined, can do little to promote active citizenship in the political sense, but they play a valuable role in stimulating a thriving civil society. The state's long-standing encroachments on the professional arts weaken their potential to encourage active citizenship and their desire to enhance the social impact of creative participation is endangering the independence of amateur or voluntary and community-based practice.

Governments should resist as far as possible the simple maintenance of a network of cultural institutions, and should direct the main thrust of their subsidies towards the fostering of creative participation by citizens. They should seek to reposition these institutions closer to where they used to be—in the state-free territory of civil society. In encouraging community and educational development the aim should be to establish free-standing participatory arts groups—and avoid creating another parallel network of public provision in the amateur sector.

Through the new information technologies, a new, more interactive relationship with attenders should be fostered and creative engagement with the arts and the cultural heritage encouraged. The national curriculum should pay greater attention to inculcating in their students creative as well as academic skills, partly to help to ensure Britain's economic competitiveness and partly to enable them to become effective and informed citizens.

Global, national and local developments are proceeding with such dizzying speed that governments are no longer able to claim to master them any more than they can the shifting aspirations of their populations. Their task is to facilitate rather than control, to enable rather than to patronise. In the arts the old Keynesian habits of top-down intervention are not so appropriate as they may have been in the past. To use a military metaphor, the question is no longer how to raise, equip and train a small but effective professional army, but how to satisfy the requirements of a *levée en masse* or a nation of home militias.

The Arts Council's old watchword, 'We know what you need; here it is and we hope you like it' will have to yield to another more permissive one, 'We know what you like; so how can we help you do it as well as possible?' This suggests that the funding bureaucracy, when it finds itself responding to the creativity of citizens rather than focusing on the needs of a creative elite, will be well-advised to adopt a humbler, more responsive attitude. It will be a revolutionary change of heart and mind. But success will not only extend creative practice among the population, but will also reinforce the cause of active citizenship.

Notes

1 Su Braden, *Artists and People*, London, Henley and Boston, Routledge and Kegan Paul, 1978. p. 133.
2 Salvador Giner, *Civil Society and its Future*. Keynote address, European Round Table of the CIRCLE Network, Budapest, March 1994. London 1997.
3 Cited in Robert Hutchison, and Andrew Feist, *Amateur Arts in the U.K.*, London, Policy Studies Institute, 1991. pp. 200–10.
4 J. Bishop, and P. Hoggett, *Organising Around Enthusiasms: Mutual Aid in Leisure*, London, Comedia Publishing Group, 1986.
5 *Report of a Conference on IT, Arts and Cultural Heritage*, IBM Corporation, 2000. p. 16.
6 *All Our Futures: Creativity, Culture and Education*, London, Department for Education and Employment and Department for Culture, Media and Sport, 1999. pp. 28–9.

The Media

MICHAEL BRUNSON

EVERY government, every political party, every pressure group of any kind always hopes that the media will be on its side, encouraging its aims, critical only in the manner of a friend who speaks his or her mind simply to be supportive. Sometimes that process advances far beyond mere hope, to become direct action. One of the first moves by the leaders of any *coup d'etat* is to seize control of the radio and television station. All totalitarian regimes try to a greater or lesser degree to ensure that an uncontrolled media does not undermine their power, authority and political bases. Often intimidation or outright control of the press and broadcasting organisations is enough. If it isn't, such regimes will usually seek to take direct control of the flow of information through its own newspapers and broadcasting outlets, frequently citing the principle of the greater good of the people as they do so. Not for nothing is China's state-controlled newspaper called *The People's Daily*.

Yet almost every example of such media control, undertaken, in name at least, by the people for the people, has been, or continues to be held in disdain, not to mention outright contempt, by considerable sections of the very people it seeks to inform. *Pravda*, once the official organ of the Soviet Union, was an object of ridicule even in its heyday. Now, reduced to being the sectarian news-sheet of the Russian Communist Party, it is largely ignored; its name, though, lives on as an instant symbol of propaganda pure and simple. Where there is no free press, somebody somewhere will almost always try to create one. One of the unforgettable experiences for anyone who was in Poland during that country's struggle for independence was to see how Solidarity, the Polish trade union which became a national freedom movement, regularly printed its own underground newspaper and managed to get it distributed to large numbers of the population. Similarly, throughout every single day of the crisis in Bosnia, and even when the bombing and shooting was at its height, a group of journalists in Sarajevo somehow managed to compile, print and sell a national morning newspaper. Just two examples of the ultimate in citizens' media.

The fact is, however, that without the spur of war or revolution attempts to recreate such mass media outlets, produced by the people for the people, have a poor track record. In Britain, mention the *Daily Worker* and you risk only a patronising smile among most working journalists, and, I suspect, the newspaper-buying public, as they remember the newspaper of the British Communist party, though its successor, the *Morning Star* survives, and is even claiming recently a rise in circulation. And who now remembers *Reynolds' News*, the Sunday paper which used to be the official organ of the

Published by Blackwell Publishers, 108 Cowley Road, Oxford OX4 1JF, UK and 350 Main Street, Malden, MA 02148, USA

Co-operative Party? So complain as we may about the failings of our national media, one thing is clear. Any attempt to force it to adopt any kind of good citizenship agenda is doomed to failure. We may bemoan our media's present practices, but as a nation we value the idea of a genuinely free press far too highly to try to impose such an agenda upon it. The recent history of the attempt to introduce curbs on the media through a privacy law only serves to underline the point.

What People Want to Read

Those in charge of our national newspapers argue that far from being oblivious of their responsibilities towards ordinary people, they are keenly aware of them, not least because, they argue, if they fail to produce what people want to read, nobody will buy their publications and they will go out of business. They also make the obvious point that every responsible newspaper is, first and foremost, in the business of publishing accurate news, or well-founded predictions of news, thus taking seriously the duty of keeping people informed about matters which affect their daily lives.

Sometimes, newspapers will take on what they see as a very active and direct citizenship role by challenging received wisdom or even the law of the land as they do so. The *News of the World*, for example, would certainly make that claim over its decision to publish the names and addresses of known paedophiles, even though it was eventually persuaded that such a campaign was creating more problems than it solved. The *Daily Mail* would certainly claim to have been upholding good citizenship when it named those it believed responsible for Stephen Lawrence's murder, or again, when it offered a large reward for information about the killing of Damilola Taylor. But those examples apart, is there any evidence of newspapers responding directly to the idea of a more active citizen culture? I believe that there is, and in the so-called 'red-top' tabloids, too. The *Sun*, for example, has hugely increased the space it devotes to political coverage in recent months. Admittedly, much of that coverage is driven by that newspaper's (and its proprietor's) implacable opposition to Britain joining the Single European Currency. You can, however, hardly accuse the *Sun* these days of failing to provoke or stimulate political discussion, even though some evidence is beginning to emerge that the paper is suffering a drop in circulation as a result of doing so. Despite that, the *Sun* appears ready to continue the trend, as its recent full-page editorial, airing its views on the position of Michael Portillo, makes clear. I do wish, however, that, at the same time, it could move one step further down the road to increased gravitas, and finally abandon its page three girls.

Cause or Effect?

When it comes to the broadsheets, they too appear to be responding more readily to the needs of those who wish to be active citizens. Both *The Times* and the *Daily Telegraph* have recently increased the space they devote to political reporting; for example, by restoring coverage of Parliament itself. I also notice an increasing readiness in such papers to set out, often with commendable clarity, the essential background to major news stories. A full-page feature in the *Telegraph*, just ahead of the recent EU summit in Nice, is a case in point. It set out very clearly the member countries' positions on the issues to be discussed, and some excellent graphics helped to make every-thing even clearer. It is in this area of background explanation, of education through information, that newspapers and the media generally can best respond to progress towards a more active citizen culture. It is no good expecting a top-down approach to all this, either by the media outlets themselves, or by those who regulate them. Stern editorials urging us to be good citizens, or any attempt to lay down agendas for the media, are not the way forward.

The old formula laid down by Lord Reith for the BBC, that it should 'inform, educate and entertain', still remains as good a blueprint as any for the media as a whole, particularly when the media itself is expanding so rapidly. We are most certainly not short of information already, nor of the means of receiving that information. It was ITN's proud boast as it unveiled its all-news channel, with its high-tech link to Wap phones, that there were ten different ways in all that the new ITN service could be accessed. Across the whole spectrum of the media in the next five to ten years that information flow will increase still further, with the steady growth of cable and satellite television, with better quality digital radio and the further expansion of the Internet.

Yet as the flow of information increases, so does the need for explanation and analysis of news and information. Every twist and turn of any major story is available to us, yet how often are we left with the feeling that we don't really know what is going on? During the crisis on the railways following the Hatfield train disaster, the media was very good at telling us how bad things were, and how it was all the result of over-reaction by Railtrack to the state of the track. It was much less good at explaining how the breakdown of communications between Railtrack and its maintenance contractors, and between Railtrack and the various regulatory bodies like the Health and Safety Executive, was making things much worse.

Quality, not Quantity

A revived sense of involved citizenship is going to need better, rather than more information. As citizenship education begins to take hold, so will the pressure for higher quality reporting from a generation armed with increased awareness of its rights and responsibilities as citizens. At a recent colloquium organised by the Citizenship Foundation, a group of young people from Hampstead Comprehensive School told us how they had watched the whole of Tony Blair's speech to the Labour Party conference, and had then studied the way the media had reported it. They were highly critical of what they had read, seen or heard in the media about the speech in particular and political reporting in general. They were annoyed because they felt that space given to the really important political issues was cut back to allow reporting of such things as Tony Blair's sweaty shirt or the yah-boo behaviour of the House of Commons.

We must not give too much weight to the views of just one group of highly motivated and articulate students. But I believe that the media should continue a trend which I sense is already under way by giving high quality explanation of the facts as well as the facts themselves. It does not have to be overly academic or heavy going. In the United States, the newspaper *USA Today* scatters 'boxes' of short briefing notes adjacent to the major stories throughout the publication. Some years ago in this country, the *Daily Mirror* used to run a feature called Mirrorscope, which provided just such background reporting in an approachable way. On a different level, the *Economist* used to carry an excellent Schools Briefing page, which I suspect was read by many more people than the students for whom it was primarily designed. Perhaps it is time now for such features to return.

It is certainly time for television news to return to what it used to do on a regular basis. Both BBC News and ITN used to carry 'backgrounders' relevant to the main stories of the day, immediately after the straight reporting of those stories. They still do to an extent, but too often the supposed explanatory pieces fail to carry the main story forward in a genuine way. Sometimes they are simply 'the story so far' or 'new viewers begin here' exercises—an excuse for retrieving the sexiest clips of videotape from the library and showing them again. On other occasions, space that could be used for well-researched and informative background reports is devoted to a 'two-way' with a correspondent that adds little that is new.

Too often what appears on the bulletins in the name of background reports is, in fact, 'lifestyle' reporting. The packages concentrate on particular examples of a given story—concentrating, for example, on individual men and women, or families, as they struggle to cope with the floods or the chaos on the trains or the bad weather. Of course, those reports have their place, and as human beings we are always interested in the trials and tribulations of our fellow men and women. It is all part of the current pressure to make television news ever more 'viewer-friendly'. We relate more easily to the experiences of other people to a given situation than to explanations of what that situation is really about. But we should never lose sight of the need to set out what is at the heart of a story and what is really going on, especially at a time when the spin-doctor is king. So in addition to the stories of how Mrs X and Mr Y are coping with the floods and the trains, we need more reports which tell us, for example, how and why local authorities are ignoring planning guidance about building on flood plains, or why it takes so long for a train operating company to produce and implement an emergency timetable. Mrs X and Mr Y, as well as the rest of us, need to know why we are being forced to cope with a crisis at all.

The New Technologies

If, therefore, it is true that there is a growing awareness that an active citizen is a well-informed citizen, and vice-versa, that is plainly something which, for its own survival, the media would do well to respond to. Once again, there are growing signs that newspapers, radio and television have sensed that a change is under way. You can see it, for example, in the way that the traditional media outlets have come to realise that they need to work with, rather than in opposition to, the latest and fastest-growing source of information, the Internet.

The Internet allows the active citizen who is familiar with its workings free and equal access to many of the very same primary sources with which the media itself works—and at almost the same time. The same Parliamentary Bills or Select Committee Reports, the same findings by a Royal Commission or Committee of Enquiry, the same White or Green Papers on which the media is reporting—all are now speedily available to those with Internet access, if (and it's a very big if) they have the time and skill to know where to look. Once again, there are signs that what we must now call 'old media' are increasingly aware that new media sources like the Internet are something to work with, rather than against.

Increasingly, newspapers are giving details of relevant websites at the foot of their reports, inviting the reader to take a look for himself at the original sources that form the basis of the paper's reporting of the story. In addition, the e-mail addresses of the correspondents and other writers responsible for such stories often now appear at the foot of the relevant article. Of course, that may mean that those journalists find themselves ever more frequently subject to the Hampstead School students' attack—the charge that their reporting bears little relation to the original sources. That, however, may be no bad thing.

Many news organisations are extending the idea of direct links with the world wide web still further—for example, the *Electronic Telegraph*, the online version of the *Daily Telegraph*, provides single click links to the relevant primary sources. You can read a summary of the findings of, say, a Royal Commission, and then, with a simple click of the mouse, go directly to the document itself.

It is not just newspapers which are providing such a service. All the main radio and television broadcasters have their own websites, and many provide the same service of direct links to material that has been the subject of their broadcasts. In addition, for example, the excellent BBC News site often offers for wider public consumption some of the background material it has acquired as it works on major stories. It is the sort of information which its specialist correspondents have gathered, and for which there may not have been room in the broadcast bulletins. Thanks to the Internet, that effort is not wasted and the material can still be made available to a wider public. When Austria, for example, was being painted as the pariah of Europe, it was on the BBC News site that I found by far the best and most detailed profile of that country's controversial politician Jörg Haider. It came, I was delighted to discover, complete with details of all the remarks from his speeches that were causing so much trouble.

Of the media tools that can encourage a more active citizenship, the Internet has the potential to be the most valuable, not least because of the vast archive it can carry. It places quite literally at the fingertips of each one of us a huge reference library, provided we can find our way around it. Every kind of public document and the details of hundreds of thousands of decisions at international, national, regional and local level are there. One of the most interesting developments is the growth of local, community based sites, where, often at parish or town council level, decisions are discussed or challenged. Active citizenship is, after all, often at its most intense at a very local level.

Incidentally, such is the welter of information available that there is an urgent need, in my view, for some kind of world-wide Internet Telephone Directory cum Yellow Pages and, ironically, it probably needs to be on paper. Trawling the search engines can be a long and frustrating business for information that you have a very strong hunch is out there somewhere, but which you somehow just cannot find. Indeed it was purely by chance that I stumbled across the new and highly innovative website of an organisation called Citizen Connect (www.citizenconnect.com). It's designed to help those who wish to change their jobs, or indeed almost anything about their whole lifestyle, by setting out for them exactly what help is available and how they can go about getting it from a multitude of official and other sources. The site itself talks of providing good quality information 'to equip individuals to move from exclusion to inclusion in employment and learning.'

Like so many of the initiatives connected with a growing awareness of citizenship, it is a bottom up and not a top-down operation. It is not simply a link to information handed down from on high. Indeed, the Managing Director of Citizen Connect, Bronwen Robinson, is particularly keen that her organisation should become a two-way street, where ordinary people inform government as much as the other way round. 'We hope we shall be able to demonstrate to the Government, by the way the website is used,' she says, 'precisely what it is that people are really looking for when they seek to change their lives, rather than the Government simply making its own judgements about what's required.' Users answer a questionnaire, and from there, the site makes an assessment of where the most useful information is likely to be, and links the user to them. It is connected, say its organisers, to a staggering 600,000 databases. It's a classic example of the way the new media can empower the citizen directly, without the need for any other intermediary, though the site also provides access to counsellors should a user need one. Citizen Connect's site has been up and running since the end of 2000. In its first three months, it had already provided access to information for 50,000 people, either directly or through employers, trade unions and other organisations who participate in the scheme.

Lastly the BBC

Alongside the new media, traditional media will have a vital part to play for many years to come. I have already referred to the BBC's website, so I close with some final thoughts about the BBC as a whole. The way in which it is financed through the licence fee (to which there still seems to be remarkably little public opposition) which in turn has led to a special sort of public regulation of, and accountability by, the BBC, has produced a very precious resource. The BBC is able to be, and indeed is dedicated to being, a public service broadcaster, in a way that the commercial broadcasters are not. That is not to say that the commercial broadcasters do not recognise and fulfil their public service obligations. Indeed, the law directly lays some of those obligations upon them. As the row over News at Ten showed, ITV, for example, is expressly required under the terms of the 1990 Broadcasting Act to schedule a high-quality bulletin of national and international news during peak viewing times. (I have to say that life would have been a great deal simpler these past two or three years had the Act gone on to specify exactly what those times were.) It came as a considerable surprise, therefore, to learn that no such formal requirement about news broadcasting is at present laid upon the BBC. The recent Broadcasting White Paper suggests that is an omission, which should be speedily put right. Indeed, the White Paper lays down important markers, not just about the whole future of broadcasting in Britain, but about the role and function of the BBC, which may help to strengthen the Corporation's primary role as a public service broadcaster. That in turn may lead to an increasingly direct role for the BBC in a citizenship culture, through, for example, the establishment of a new BBC outlet that is devoted purely to education. It is a project which is known to be close to the heart of Lord Puttnam, the former film producer who is now the chairman of the Government's new General Teaching Council, and one of Tony Blair's education advisers. Such an operation could be of enormous help as we seek to get citizenship education under way in all our schools.

It is, though, through *good quality information* which educates us all, of whatever age, that the media—old and new—can play a most valuable role in the promotion of more active citizenship, though it already does a great deal more than it is given credit for. This, however, *will* be a two-way street. The more active citizens we become, the more high quality information we are likely to demand, and that is something the media is in a unique position to recognise and supply.

Citizenship and Schools

RICHARD PRING

Introduction

FROM September 2002, citizenship will be a compulsory part of the curriculum of our schools at Key Stages 3 and 4. The basis for this innovation is the 1998 Crick Report *Citizenship and the Teaching of Democracy in Schools*, published by the Qualifications and Curriculum Authority. The reason, indeed pressure, to teach Citizenship is both recent and old. Certainly, in the last few years, no doubt enhanced by a National Curriculum which focuses so much on academic attainment, there is growing concern for the neglect of those personal and social qualities which teachers have traditionally attached so much importance to: clearly, the attributes of being a good citizen would count amongst such qualities. But the Report builds on a sustained argument by Crick himself, who has constantly argued that political education is crucial to the maintenance and enhancement of the skills, understanding, and knowledge presupposed in the democratic structures of society. His concept of 'political literacy'[1] has been a powerful and influential one, though (until now) not influential enough.

On the other hand, the proposals of the Report and the implementation of these in the curriculum have not been met with universal acclaim. There are the complaints that there is no room on an already overcrowded timetable. What will go to make room for this new subject? (Already, history, geography, the arts are being squeezed out to make room for vocational alternatives at Key Stage 4.) Teachers question the acceptability of the new subject by more sceptical university tutors. Performance at Key Stage 4 will need to be assessed and graded, but are there objective measures of the moral and social qualities which are at the core of 'the good citizen'? School subjects traditionally draw upon the resources of well established bodies of knowledge, but where are such bodies of knowledge in the subject of Citizenship? And, in the absence of such an agreed academic and research-based tradition, are we not in danger of substituting the controversial opinions of teachers for well-tested bodies of knowledge, acquaintance with an understanding of which gives teachers the authority to teach? Just as Socrates asked in the *Meno* where are the teachers of virtue (and provisionally concluded that virtue cannot be taught because there are no such teachers), so, too, we might ask 'Where are the teachers of Citizenship?' (and tentatively conclude that, so far at least, none have been produced—though some education departments are boldly making the attempt).

In my view, there are answers to these questions; but such answers do require some refinement of what is being proposed. They require, too, a

Published by Blackwell Publishers, 108 Cowley Road, Oxford OX4 1JF, UK and 350 Main Street, Malden, MA 02148, USA

reappraisal of what the curriculum more generally should be about—and, indeed, would be if it were able to reclaim a tradition, within the humanities especially, which for too long has been neglected. Such answers, finally, require a re-examination of the context in which learning takes place and of the professional development of teachers, which too often are neglected as learning is seen to be no more than a function of individual teaching acts.

The Humanities

Performance indicators (whereby schools are assessed and accorded a place in league tables, or whereby teachers are rewarded or reprimanded, or whereby the 'stakeholders' and 'clients' evaluate the services provided) become quite understandably the targets themselves. The distinction becomes blurred between the educational aims and the indications that such aims have been achieved—just as, in the past, there was often a confusion between intelligence and the scores on intelligence tests. The aims, the purposes of teaching the humanities, lie intrinsically, not in the passing of examinations in the humanities. The examination results are but indicators that there is the deeper understanding, the breadth of knowledge, the personal skills and qualities which one would like to see emerging from a study of literature, history, drama, philosophy, geography, and the arts. But, in the context wherein performance indicators are confused with aims (and thus become the targets), it is easy to lose sight of the *educational* purpose of these studies.

This was not always so. Indeed, at a time when schools were less obsessive about league tables, performance indicators, and examinations, they were able to address the questions about the real value of a liberal and humane education for the very young people for whom examinations were seen to be mostly irrelevant. The raising of the school-leaving age in the early 1970s was one such moment. The temptation was to put on vocational courses, to provide a training in skills which would make otherwise alienated young people economically useful. But the temptation was resisted as teachers re-addressed the real purposes of teaching the humanities—helping the young people become 'more human' and (in the words of the Schools Council[2]) enabling the teachers to emphasise their common humanity with the pupils and their common uncertainty in the face of significant and personal problems. It was the view of so many teachers that the kinds of issues that concerned young people—even those who by normal standards were ineducable—were in fact the very stuff of good literature, drama, history, geography, social studies and the arts. Envy, jealousy, justice, the use and abuse of power, violence, revenge, relations with authority, relations between the sexes were as much the themes of Shakespeare as they were the conversation pieces of the teenagers. Teaching at its best was, and is, the mediation of that literary, historical, artistic culture to the personal concerns and explorations of the young. We saw, then, the development of curriculum to reflect that view of teaching and the power of the humanities—the 'Humanities Curriculum

Project', 'Geography for the Young School Leaver', 'History 13–16', Social Studies, and (from America) 'Man: A Course of Study'.

It is a sad fact that, living in an age when the history of education began or was revised in 1986, little or no reference is made to the creative thinking which in the 1970s addressed the same sort of issues which the present proposals for citizenship education are intended to deal with. Then, too, there was concern about the alienation of young people, requiring a curriculum which was (and was felt to be) relevant to their needs, but which, not resorting to the merely useful or vocational, addressed the values and questions which are central to living a responsible life as a citizen within a democratic framework.

There were, and remain, three crucial aspects to this. They are, first, the curriculum content; second, the mode of teaching; third, the context in which the curriculum should be taught. Of course, these are inseparable—pedagogy, the method of teaching, is integral to the subject matter being taught. But, artificial though it may be, I need for purposes of argument to examine each separately.

Content

I take as a first example Bruner's 'Man: A Course of Study'.[3] It was an innovative curriculum within the social studies broadly conceived. It centred around three questions. What is it that makes us human? How did we become so? How might we be more so? In answering these questions, Bruner picked out five features which make us distinctively human—the prolonged childhood, the acquisition of language, the use of tools, the formation of social groups, and the creation of myths through which one gives meaning to one's life. The curriculum aimed at enabling young people to explore these distinctive features, to make sense of them by drawing upon the resources of linguistics, anthropology, sociology, political studies, etc. These were the cultural sources upon which deliberations were based and opinions put to the test. The young people were entering into explorations which had no definitive end, no final conclusion, no social consensus—but disciplined by argument and by evidence. Such explorations would be made possible by acquaintance with, and understanding of, the key ideas through which these different kinds of knowledge and disciplines of thinking were organised. Such key ideas could, according to Bruner,[4] be put across to any child at any age in an intellectually respectable form—though translated into the particular 'mode of representation' of those children.

I shall return to the significance and relevance of this in the next section, but here it is worth noting that a curriculum was conceived in which key concepts were identified through which the most important questions of human identity and development might be explored. No political education worth its name can cut itself off from such aspiration and concern—and yet they are the very subject matter of the humanities.

The second example is drawn from the 'Humanities Curriculum Project'.[5] Again, the content was, as it were, the issues which most concern and yet divide society—the existence and tolerance of poverty, the use of violence to pursue just ends, the treatment and nurturing of young persons, the pursuit of justice and fairness, the conditions of a just war, the dignity of employment, the rights of those in authority, the relations between the sexes. In an open and democratic society, consensus cannot be expected. But disagreements have to be dealt with rationally, with respect for the other's thought out views, with tolerance of differences, with reference to relevant evidence. Hence, the deliberations of the students should be evidence based—and the content of the curriculum (or at least the resources upon which the curriculum draws) should be the relevant texts and artefacts, which articulated the considered views, the evidence, the arguments upon which the deliberations might draw. Such resources would, of course, include the tracts of political philosophers, the examples of 'political art', the arguments of politicians, the accounts of wars, rebellions and reconciliation. The approach was described well in the following way.

The problem is to give every man some access to a complex cultural inheritance, some hold on his personal life and on his relationships with the various communities to which he belongs, some extension of his understanding of, and sensitivity towards, other human beings. The aim is to forward understanding, discrimination and judgment in the human field—it will involve reliable, factual knowledge, where this is appropriate, direct experience, imaginative experience, some appreciation of the dilemmas of the human condition, of the rough hewn nature of many of our institutions, and some rational thought about them. (Schools Council, op. cit., para. 6)

The crucial factors were: first, the centrality of those themes which, shaped by conflicting values, divided people from each other; secondly, the careful presentation of ideas and evidence through which those conflicts could be explored and possibly resolved; thirdly, the pedagogical skills through which such exploration might be advanced; and, finally, the context in which that might best take place.

Pedagogy

To be a citizen entails certain rights and responsibilities. Those would include the right to participate in the deliberations which affect personal and social well-being at different levels of society. Such deliberations are crucial where consensus is lacking over important matters which affect that well-being—and where there seem to be no agreed ways of resolving the differences of opinion. Responsibilities are rarely as well defended as rights, but the democratic institutions and procedures which protect those rights require constant vigilance, lest they be eroded by those who are able to exercise power. Hence, a responsibility upon the citizenry to ensure the preservation of those institutions and those procedures.

Such responsibilities are not readily accepted or exercised. They require certain dispositions or civic virtues. They require social and personal skills. They require a basic understanding of the development of the social and political framework in which one lives and works. Such dispositions, skills and understating can and should be the aims of education—and thus have a place in the curriculum. However, the emphasis in the past has too often been upon the 'understanding'—a crucial, albeit not the sole, element in such an educational preparation.

I wish, therefore, to focus on the first two—the dispositions and the skills. But acknowledgement must be made of the kind of understanding which Crick has so effectively argued for over two decades. His concept of 'political literacy' referred to a grasp of those ideas or concepts without which one would not be able to understand events from a political point of view. Just as in the physical and biological sciences, there are key organising concepts through which experience is organised in a particular way and explanatory theories developed, so, too, in the social sciences. Key concepts or ideas shape our thought, structure our understanding, enable us to explain and make predictions. Without a grasp of such key ideas, we fail to see significant elements or make sense of what is happening. The school curriculum, in its different disciplinary components, should be structured around those key ideas which give insight into what otherwise would remain mysterious, unintelligible, and thus beyond our control.

Furthermore, as is argued by Bruner, such key ideas can be acquired at varying levels of abstraction. There are ever deeper understandings of those ideas. The concept of 'power', and of its exercise in social groups, is one which can be grasped in an elementary form at a very early age. But we know that, through experience and reflection upon that experience, such a concept becomes more significant, more sophisticated, and indeed more articulated through theoretical development. This 'spiral curriculum'—the constant returning to key, organising concepts at deeper levels of representation—is essential to that political understanding at the heart of citizenship education. And this is achieved through the interaction between experience, text (dramatic, literary, political, historical) and the struggle 'to make sense' under the guidance of a good teacher.

What we do know from that earlier work in the humanities is that such development requires, on the whole, a distinctive approach to learning—and thus to teaching—something not fully recognised in the Crick Report. Such learning is a struggle to make sense of the social world which is shaped by values. Such values are essentially controversial—that is, they in fact do not have universal agreement and there is not, as is the case in science, agreement over the method by which disagreements might be resolved. Such a struggle to understand, to make sense, to come to conclusions (for conclusions must be arrived at in areas of practical living), requires the development of particular dispositions, qualities, and skills. It requires, too, the development in the teacher of particular skills and qualities very different from those exercised in more transmission modes of teaching.

Central to such deliberation must be discussion—the readiness to articulate one's thoughts and feelings, to expose them to the critical scrutiny of others and to test them out against the evidence. This is by no means easy. Indeed, it requires the development of habits and dispositions which go against the grain. Our natural tendency is not to seek critical scrutiny of others, not to test our opinions against the evidence. Our natural tendency is to defend our view, and (where necessary) resort to the irrational modes of dealing with contrary views—shouting, using sarcasm, belittling, ignoring evidence which casts doubt on favoured opinions. To develop the spirit of exploration, the readiness to seek others' views, the questioning of ready-made assumptions needs to be carefully and steadily nurtured. There is also need for the readiness to listen to others—and the interactive social skills of so listening. It is important to distinguish between respect for the person who holds an opinion and the opinion itself—have respect for each who sincerely puts forward an opinion or argument, even where the opinion is otiose and the argument invalid.

The significance of this cannot be overestimated. There are certain social skills which we often take for granted, but which have in fact been developed in specific social contexts, in particular, within families who eat together, discuss, question prevailing values, challenge unsubstantiated claims, justify their views when subjected to criticism. But there are many young people who have never experienced such a social context or such social interaction—who, for example, have rarely if ever enjoyed the normal interactions which occur over a family meal (a fifth of households have no table around which such family meals can be taken).

Therefore, central to political education (and thus to the development of citizenship in schools) is the well organised discussion, in which controversial issues which divide people in society are explored, opinions are articulated and defended on the basis of evidence, respect is given to those of contrary views, the search for truth is fostered, but the tolerance of diversity and of uncertainty promoted. The skills and dispositions for so engaging are not easy to acquire, and yet they are either taken for granted or regarded as unimportant in a curriculum which too often pursues a narrow form of academic excellence and a pedagogy which relies on the transmission of unquestioned knowledge.

Teachers, also, frequently lack the skills and understanding to promote such learning. It requires specific teaching skills and dispositions—the protection of minority views even where these might be extreme, the encouragement of the holders of their views to base them on evidence and argument, the promotion of rationality, the provision of the cultural resources (the literature, the political arguments, the historical accounts) which relate to the controversial issues being explored, capacity to listen and to help the students articulate more effectively their opinions, the tolerance of differences, the sharing of uncertainty. Such teachers must know when and where their own views promote or inhibit exploration—when and where the exercise of authority gets in the way of learning. Indeed, the exercise of authority requires much careful consideration, for, in matters of controversial values, there is ultimately no authority over what should or should not be believed. Rather is the teacher's authority one that is concerned with the protection of appropriate procedures for the proper, open, evidence-based discussion of important issues.

How to discuss and explore controversial issues which affect profoundly the quality of our personal and social lives is central to preparation for citizenship. And yet this remains a weakness of the Crick Report, speaking as it did from the quite substantial research and evaluation that has been undertaken. It confuses the neutral stance of the teacher with regard to controversial issues with an indifference to values, as though such a teacher would have to pose as a moral eunuch. But that should never be the case. A neutral role would be adopted as a pedagogical device, to be tested against experience, whereby the authority position of the teacher does not inhibit the expression and exploration of views by the student. Such a role, essential on pedagogical not moral grounds, receives little or no attention in the proliferating programmes and prescriptions for citizenship education.

Context

Education—its aims and purposes, its content, how it should be delivered and evaluated—is itself a controversial matter. It concerns the proper bringing up and nurturing of the next generation, judgements about what is valuable to protect and to promote, concerns about the influences which young people are exposed to. As such, it will ever be the subject of argument and disagreement—with advocates engaged in disputes about the quality of life to be pursued through particular social and school arrangements, as well as through pedagogical styles and curriculum content. In engaging in such an educational debate, so one is able to draw upon philosophical works, sociological analyses, psychological claims about intelligence or motivation. The study of education does itself draw upon the humane studies, requires the careful articulation of purposes and values and the means of attaining and embodying those values. And, indeed, as Bruner pointed out in 'Man: A Course of Study', a study of education (its aims, values, and organisation) should be a component of the social studies curriculum—indeed, of the preparation to be a citizen.

However, it is odd, indeed, if such freedom (informed, of course, and systematically pursued), though accorded to the students by reason of the controversial nature of the subject matter, were not accorded to the teachers for the very same reason. The teachers are, themselves, the custodians of those values which are central to the preparation of young people for living intelligently in a society where there is lack of consensus in matters of profound human concern. Teachers, themselves, must embody the very values, dispositions and skills which they are trying to nurture in their students. They, themselves, need to be engaged in the very exploration of those values which permeate their work—and which cannot be arbitrated by any superior authority. They inherit an educational tradition—a conversation between the generations—in which ideas are explored, values questioned, conclusions tentatively reached and later refined through further argument and evidence.

If there is to be education for citizenship, in which people learn to participate in the deliberation of the values which shape society, then the deliberations of the teachers themselves need to be taken seriously. The schools need to be seen less as institutions for delivering a curriculum (the government's curriculum), and more as forums wherein ideas are explored and proposals shared amongst the teachers and between teachers and students. To engage in such deliberations, teachers need the framework in which they can bring their experience and reflection to bear upon some of the most intractable problems of society, namely, how to nurture and educate the next generation of citizens in a world which knows few certainties, but which must find ways of living hopefully in a society which embraces different modes of living and valuing.

This is not fanciful thinking. In establishing the Schools Council in 1964, its chief architect Derek Morrell saw the 'educational crisis' to be part of 'a general crisis of values' and education (and the curriculum) as 'contributing to a solution of this crisis of values'.[6] That contribution lay in enabling the teachers, in partnership with others in the community, to explore the impact of the massive changes, especially in values, which were impacting upon society and affecting institutions and relationships within them. Unless the impact of such changes is explored by society, teachers and students, drawing upon the very best resources we have inherited (not as dictating the future but as entering into our deliberations about the future), then what is citizenship education about, other than an initiation into the values and understandings of the past without acknowledging their limitations for the future?

Furthermore, there was then a flourishing of institutions and teachers' centres where such deliberations took place and where curriculum responses to those changes were developed—changes in the teaching of geography, history, literature and drama so as to enable young people to participate in an informed manner in those controversial issues which were central to their and to others' lives. Promoting citizenship in our schools without addressing the broader institutional framework will lead these studies to yet another sterile and cerebral exercise.

Conclusion

John Stuart Mill in his *Essay on Liberty* (1859) (surely a resource to be made accessible to all young people as, through the humanities, they examine what it means to be human and to create institutions which respect that humanity) said

the peculiar evil of silencing the expression of opinion is that it is robbing the human race; posterity as well as the existing generation; those who dissent from the opinion, still more than those who hold it. If the opinion is right, they are deprived of the opportunity of exchanging error for truth: if wrong, they lose, what is almost as great a benefit, the clearer perception and livelier impression of the truth, produced by its collision with error. (p. 143)

It is a sentiment which applies to the classroom where students seek to question received opinions on matters which affect them closely. It applies to schools where teachers want to question the official doctrines which shape their teaching. It applies to the wider society which must always hold up to scrutiny the public and professional services whereby young lives are formed and values promoted. The alternative is to assume certainties where there is room for doubt, authority where there are no sure foundations for it, consensus where there are in fact conflicting values.

But taking Mill seriously—essential in the development of citizens in a pluralist and democratic society—requires serious attention to the skills, the procedural values, the virtues and dispositions which need to be developed in young people. It requires, too, the respect for the right of teachers to enter seriously into the deliberations of the very educational values which are imparted to their students. And it requires the context—in school and outside—where such 'expressions of opinion' are allowed and encouraged, and enabled to develop through criticism and evidence. We have a long way to go before there can be genuine education for citizenship.

Notes

1 B. Crick, in Crick, B. & Heater, D., eds., *Essays on Political Education*, London: Falmer Press 1997.
2 Schools Council Working Paper No 2, *Raising the School Leaving Age*, London: HMSO, 1965.
3 Paper in J. Bruner, *Towards a Theory of Instruction*, Cambridge, Mass, Harvard University Press, 1965.
4 J. Bruner, *The Process of Education* Cambridge, Mass, Harvard University Press 1960.
5 See L. Stenhouse, *Authority, Education and Emancipation*, London: Heinemann, 1975.
6 D. Morrell, *Education and Change*, The Annual Joseph Payne Memorial Lecture, 1965/6, London: College of Preceptors, 1967.

The Need for Lifelong Learning

TOM SCHULLER

'Education is one of the most important predictors—usually, in fact, *the* most important predictor—of many forms of social participation—from voting to associational
membership, to chairing a local committee to hosting a dinner party to giving blood
. . . Education is an especially powerful predictor of participation in public, formally
organised activities.'[1]

ROBERT Putnam's conclusion is unambiguous, and is confirmed by many
other studies across the world. However we define citizenship, it is closely
related to education. But what is the nature of that relationship? Does its
omnipresence simply mean that the more we stack up years of schooling the
more active our citizenry will be? Inevitably it's a lot more complicated than
that. In this chapter I begin with the notion of social capital, dramatically
popularised by Putnam in the last few years, because it enables us to think
more broadly about the relationship between education and citizenship. At
the very least we need to take stock of how far the expansion of formal
education is the royal road to strengthening that relationship; I take a definite
position against the further prolongation of initial formal education, propos-
ing instead that we need many more alternative channels for learning. I
introduce, as a basis for discussion, the framework produced by a recent
report on citizenship education, chaired by this volume's editor. Some policy
proposals conclude.

It is not only those of us who work in educational institutions who would
be disappointed if there were not a strong relationship between education and
active citizenship. Cynics but not many others would be happy to find that
people who engaged in learning were apathetic abstainers from political life,
broadly construed. Intuitively a more schooled populace, with access to a
huge range of information sources, should be more inclined to participate in
debate and decisions on whichever of the policy areas most took their fancy.
Yet consider this dystopic possibility: we become so persuaded of the
advantages that education brings to our individual career prospects, so
convinced of the meritocratic possibilities offered by a knowledge economy
and so pressed for time converting our enhanced human capital into material
advancement that we concentrate all our efforts on our careers, perhaps also
on getting our children off to a good start. What little time we have left over is
spent relaxing in front of the television, now supplier of an infinity of
fragmented viewing choice. No time is allocated to doing the kinds of
things which would recognisably make up a citizenship culture. An educated
population, yes, even a skilled and competent one; but not an educated
citizenry.

The reassuring evidence is that there is for the most part a direct

Published by Blackwell Publishers, 108 Cowley Road, Oxford OX4 1JF, UK and 350 Main Street, Malden, MA 02148, USA

relationship between education and active citizenship. The mid-1980s survey by Parry and colleagues of a representative sample of about 1500 people in the UK covered several modes of participation: voting, contacting political representatives, collective action of various kinds, party campaigning and direct action. Their general conclusion[2] was that there is 'a relatively strong linear progression in levels of participation from the bottom of the educational ladder to the top'. The more education one receives, the more likely one is to engage in most forms of mild political activity. Even when mediating factors such as wealth are taken into account, the relationship remains. Voting was the only mode to deviate from the pattern, for reasons we don't need to go into here.

However, Parry's survey revealed no trends over time, whether participation was increasing or decreasing. And it was of political participation, which would on its own be a narrow conception of citizenship. A broader conception includes levels of involvement in a range of other activities or organisations, and attitudes towards one's social environment, for example in the extent to which one trusts one's fellow citizens. These are the kinds of factors used to measure social capital.

Social capital is a concept with deep historical roots but a relatively recent political profile.[3] Its definitions are too manifold and applications too diverse to list here, but in essence it refers to social networks and the associated norms of trust and reciprocity which give the networks value and efficacy. Its most prominent proponent is Robert Putnam (*op. cit.*), who has drawn together a remarkable range of information to chart the patterns of social capital in the US during the last century. Putnam's general case is that there has been a long-term decline in most forms of civic participation in the US, in spite of a substantial growth in educational levels. How can this be? The short answer is that the decline would have been even steeper if education hadn't expanded, but that education on its own has not been effective enough to counter the corrosion of social capital. The most acidic constituent of the corrosion is identified by Putnam as television, which gobbles up time in ways that destroy human association. The formal and informal networks that tie people together, constitute social capital and accompany and promote particular forms of civic engagement are fraying badly. Putnam is neither a pessimist nor passive—he believes that the trend is reversible and is actively engaged in developing networks for civic engagement in the US; but he marshals a formidable array of data to show how far participation levels have fallen, from church membership to the organised bowling clubs which gave his book its striking title. From this angle, education has been shoring up a crumbling political edifice, not sculpting a fine new civic body.

Measures of Participation

Evidence on levels of social capital in the UK is more mixed. Some forms of participation appear to be in decline, with falling levels of participation in elections at every level, and increasing indications of cynicism towards public office-holders. Some of the strongest traditional forms of engagement are crumbling, such as the solidarity of trade unionism. However the latest report from the annual British Social Attitudes survey shows some changes up and down, but its overall verdict is that 'there is no reason to conclude from our data that civic engagement in Britain is in any sort of crisis. On the contrary, for a sizeable segment of the population, mostly the better-off, organised local activity seems to be an integral part of their lives. The problem is that those who should have most to gain from such activity tend to be the most isolated from it—whether by choice or circumstance.'[4] This is as true for education as for access to and use of the health service and social services.

Peter Hall[5] has also argued that the case for decline cannot be substantiated. Some types of participation have declined, but others have sprouted in their place, and the overall balance sheet over the last quarter century is quite neutral. However, in his conclusions about education Hall reinforces Putnam. He identifies the rise in secondary and higher level educational achievement as one of the key drivers behind the maintenance of social capital. This is specifically linked to the rise in female educational attainment, which accounts for the closing of the gap between male and female levels of civic engagement. This is in striking contrast to the way the class gap has persisted, with members of lower socio-economic categories scoring low in educational achievement and in civic engagement. Hall reports that in the 1950s the experience of post-secondary education increased community involvement on average by about 76 per cent, compared with secondary education alone; but by 1990 this difference had increased to 110 per cent. We do not, he says, know how to account for this exactly, but it may well be the case that the expansion of higher education drew in a wider cross-section of the population, with a greater marginal effect on their propensity to engage in civic activity. 'In short, not only do greater numbers of British citizens benefit from post-secondary education today, but the average effect of higher education seems to be substantially greater than it was during the 1950s' (p. 429).

In short, education in the formal measurable sense is clearly associated with the probability of active citizenship. This must be seen as positive at a general level. However, closer analysis shows that the association between rising educational levels and civic engagement is not a smooth one. Notably, both the analyses cited above show that different social groups have benefited from educational expansion to different degrees. Most obviously, higher levels of education are associated with the better-off. They therefore support social capital, but also in some senses reinforce social divisions.

All the analyses quoted above, it should be noted, refer to formal education, and almost all to the qualifications most commonly gained in the initial period of schooling. This, I shall argue, is understandable—it is the most easily measurable which gets measured—but is a seriously outdated and misleading way of thinking about learning. It vitiates much of the analysis of human capital and should not be allowed to dominate our thinking or, indeed, public policy about learning and citizenship. Educational values can get lost in the statistical rhetoric of electoral politics.

One of the advantages of the concept of social capital is that it frees us up to think more broadly about how learning takes place and its basic purposes, and the interaction between learning and doing. The key points I wish to make are these:

- a good educational foundation is essential for an active citizenry, but this should not be confused with prolonged institutional education;
- extending the time people spend in initial education may in fact reduce their capacity to act independently and develop autonomous competences;
- we need to give far more acknowledgement and support to a wide range of informal learning.

The government plans to retain more and more young people in education, in order that they should attain at least level 2 qualifications—the *sine qua non* of effective economic participation at the individual level. This is fine; the UK still has a very long tail of wholly unqualified people lacking even basic skills, and without these participation in many walks of life is difficult—not impossible, but difficult. It is reasonable that there should be quite a sharp dividing line between the support offered to individuals up to this level, and the expectation that those proceeding to higher education should take a share of financial responsibility for their own learning. Altering the definition of the Age Participation Rate (which measures the proportions of successive cohorts that enter higher education) so that targets are expressed in terms of the 18–30 age group and not in terms of the school leaver cohort is a major step, symbolically as well as for policy guidance.

Yet expansion has for too long been treated simplistically: the more the better, as an implicit counterslogan to the reactionary 'more means worse' of the 1960s Conservatives. Amongst the middle classes, over 70 per cent of children now go on to some form of higher education. Young people's levels of dependence, on parents and the state, has been enormously extended, in spite of buoyant labour markets, which allow them access to jobs on a regular or intermittent basis, and rising levels of wealth. If education is about the whole person, it is not rational to expect institutionalised forms to supply it all. We need to think instead about how different forms of learning will enable people to be economically active, parentally competent, socially reasonable and civically engaged—not all at the same time necessarily, but at least potentially throughout their lives.

There is a major political challenge here. As the proportion of middle class children who do not go straight to university shrinks, so the pressure not to be one of the minority grows. This constituency is large and vocal. But a check on the spreading prolongation of initial education and the dependency this generates not only makes sense in efficiency terms; it should also allow a better overall balance between formal education, learning and other forms of activity—including citizenship. Here let me draw on a recently concluded research programme, funded by the ESRC on the theme of the learning society.[6] Ironically, given that the content of most of the programme concentrated on formal education and workplace training, one of the major conclusions was the need to recognise and develop those types of informal learning which account for so much of people's overall growth and development, but which are commonly squeezed out by the excessive focus on institutionalisation and measurement. As Frank Coffield, the director of the programme, has observed, policy-makers and researchers tend to pay lip service to the importance of informal learning but to ignore it in practice. Not only are we are ignoring or undervaluing fertile forms of learning. It may well be that the most publicly emphasised forms of education, and the ones which are most commonly used to measure a society's progress such as enrolment levels in higher education, are ambiguous in their impact, or even misleading. In one of the projects in the programme, John Field and I explored the relationship between the initial phase of education and the extent to which people engage in learning throughout their lives, examining interesting apparent differences between England on the one hand and Scotland and Northern Ireland on the other. On the basis of small-scale research with a number of stakeholders in different economic sectors, covering education providers as well as employers, we accumulated evidence that the impact of prolonged initial education on motivation to learn throughout life is at best ambiguous, and possibly negative (p. 109). If—and it remains to be tested over time—recent graduates are more likely to have an instrumental attitude to education, this suggests a weaker link to civic engagement.

Strikingly, OECD, for decades the leading exponent of economistic capitalism, has recently been developing its position in very significant ways in order to accommodate interaction between the economic and the social spheres. The focus on economic performance remains, but the organisation is coming to acknowledge two key things.[7] First, economic performance depends on a degree of social coherence: a country will not prosper if large segments of the population are excluded. Secondly, the development and application of skills for the much-vaunted knowledge economies are as much a function of social networks and personal relationships as they are of technical individual application. OECD's analysis explores the relationship between social and human capital, with civic engagement included as part of the definition of social capital. Although cautious in its conclusions, it gives support to the idea that education in its conventional sense will only seriously enhance skill levels if it is embedded in these wider social processes and activities. Now it would be an exaggeration to say that OECD has embraced active citizenship as a vital ingredient in a nation's economic performance, but the new line of analysis makes the idea not at all far-fetched, even within that organisation's frame of reference.

The relationships are not simple, and we should not naively assume a positive one between education, prosperity and citizenship. If Putnam's analysis is correct, the US has just gone through one of the longest booms in its history with diminishing levels of civic engagement. Prosperity may be the essential prerequisite for good social interaction and civic engagement, since material levels affect the ability and propensity to participate, rather than the other way around. Yet the conclusion on this depends on timescales. The decline in social capital may take time to make its impact felt.

Linkages

In this section I turn from general associations between education and citizenship to policy-related work specifically geared to encouraging a link between the two, by reporting on the work of an Advisory Group to the Secretary of State for Education and Employment, of which I was a member.[8] The Group was chaired by this volume's editor; its formal remit was to advise on how the principles and aims of citizenship might inform the education and training of 16–19 year olds but the discussion ranged beyond that unnecessarily tight upper age limit. The aspiration of the report (shared by its predecessor on schooling and citizenship) is ambitious: 'no less than a change in the political culture of this country both nationally and locally: for people to think of themselves as active citizens, willing, able and equipped to have an influence in public life and with the critical capacities to weigh evidence before speaking and acting; to build on and extend radically the best in existing traditions of community involvement and public service; and to make [people] . . . individually confident in finding new forms of involvement and action among themselves' (p. 4).

One key issue which ran throughout our discussions was the appropriate mix between learning *what* and learning *how*, between academic knowledge about institutions and procedures on the one hand, and the skills needed to be a citizen in practice on the other. We reached consensus on this. Rashly perhaps, we went further and tried to set out a framework for thinking about the learning outcomes. What did we think might be included? We set out our thoughts under four headings: concepts, roles, areas of knowledge, and skills. These can be summarised as follows.

Concepts:

Participation	becoming involved, for example, as an active member of a community group or organisation
Engagement	taking participation further, for example, by trying to influence the strategies or policies of the group
Advocacy	being able to put a case
Research	being able to find relevant and alternative sources of information
Evaluation	being able to judge the relative merits of different possibilities
Empathy	being able to consider an issue from the point of view of others
Conciliation	being able to resolve disagreements and conflicts

Leadership	being able to initiate and co-ordinate the agreed activities of others
Representation	being able to speak or act on behalf of others
Responsibility	thinking before one acts and accepting the consequences
Roles:	Community member; Consumer; Family member; Lifelong learner; Taxpayer; Voter; Worker.

Areas of knowledge:

- how decisions are made at local, national, European, Commonwealth and international levels and how these decisions may or may not be influenced by citizens
- how public and private services are delivered and what opportunities exist to access and influence them
- how the different communities of national, religious, ethnic or cultural identity which make up the United Kingdom relate to each other
- how equal opportunities and anti-discrimination legislation and codes of practice apply
- how policies on taxation and economic management affect individuals and groups
- the rights and responsibilities which individuals have in employment
- how each particular vocation is affected by public laws, policies and events
- the roles of individuals as family members
- the rights and responsibilities of consumers
- the different approaches to policy of the main political parties and pressure groups
- how people can contribute to the life of voluntary groups and of their local communities
- environmental issues and sustainable development

Skills:

- demonstrating an understanding of the rights and responsibilities associated with a particular role
- applying a framework of moral values relevant to a particular situation
- demonstrating an understanding of, and respect for, cultural, gender, religious, ethnic and community diversities both nationally and globally
- combating prejudice and discrimination
- critically appraising information sources (advertising, media, pressure groups, political parties) managing financial affairs
- assessing risk and uncertainty when making a decision or choice
- initiating, responding to, and managing change
- selecting the appropriate mechanisms or institutions for dealing with particular issues

- identifying the social, resource and environmental consequences of particular courses of action.
  (Source: condensed from paras 5.6–5.11 of *Citizenship for 16–19 Year Olds in Education and Training, op. cit.*)

There is no space here to do much more than relate this schema. It does seem to me to provide a useful framework for thinking about the relationship between education and citizenship. It allows us to tackle discrete but over-lapping aspects such as those identified by Nicholas Emler and Elizabeth Frazer:[9] the body of information which education imparts; the pedagogic style adopted; the organisation and governance of the educational institution; and the impact of the educational setting's informal associations. Although the report is geared primarily to policy and practice in the formal sector the framework enables us to go beyond this, to analyse the kinds of networks which Emler and Frazer suggest as particularly relevant to the educational effect on political outcomes. My point is not that the framework is definitive, more that it provides a broad base for understanding and debating the impact of education beyond the formal system. It provides a provisional template for assessing the adequacy of our systems (in the plural): how far do they meet the requirements implied, and how far do they complement each other in so doing (or failing to do so)?

Policy Implications

What directions does this line of argument suggest? Can we go further than a comfortable Whiggish expectation that the almost inexorable expansion of formal education will of itself promote a citizenship culture? I think so. First, we need to encourage a growing recognition that important learning takes place in many different contexts. The political version of this is that pluralist democracy requires plural forms of learning. This gives fresh meaning to the old, and repeatedly ignored, plea for parity of esteem. There are many types of learning which are as important if not more important than academic learning, and a citizenship culture requires these to be adequately supported. To take just one example: participation in cultural activities of the kind advocated by Anthony Everitt in his contribution to this volume is just as likely to generate a fruitful two-way relationship between learning and civic engagement as many more formal modes of learning.

Secondly, it follows from this that opportunities for learning by doing need to be given a much higher priority, rather than the further expansion of conventional opportunities. This is especially true for younger people, where motivation, and hence successful learning, follows from genuine engagement and responsibility. Maybe some of the traditional paths, such as community service, need rebranding to save them from tired connotations of dutiful activity; but voluntary work exists in a myriad of forms which could be strengthened without becoming so formalised that the purpose is defeated.

Instrumentally, employers could be far more explicit about giving credit in recruitment and promotion practices to citizenship activities, which do so much to develop the transferable skills that are putatively sought after. Symbolically, we should reform the absurdly named set of honours awards so that civic participation was visibly rewarded, and give this move the persuasive rationale that it contributes to the country's stock of human as well as social capital would be a good start.

Similarly, higher education could do much more to encourage its members—staff and students—to participate. There will be inevitable groans about overcrowded curricula leaving no space or time for such activity. These are reasonable but rarely rational, especially in an era when stocking up with information is often a short-sighted and futile activity. Universities are not community development organisations, but their relationship to the community goes well beyond an economic impact. Encouraging staff to take part in local or national civic activities would be a refreshing sign of commitment to a quite traditional mission. Of course it happens already, but there are mounting pressures squeezing out such activity. Important but limited initiatives such as Individual Learning Accounts and Investors in People could have their horizons dramatically expanded to include a wider variety of learning. ILAs, which after all entail only a tiny per capita input from the state to trigger more spending on learning on the part of the individual or the employer, should be given freer rein so that a wider variety of cultural learning is supported. Surprisingly both components of Investment in People could be taken more literally: 'investment' would cover the social returns to learning that greater civic engagement brings, whilst 'people' means what it says—i.e. citizens as well as employees, as Karen Evans states in her chapter. Maybe we could start to include social capital measures in statements of local assets, just as human capital is beginning to figure as a national asset. (On the other hand, fear Greeks bearing gifts—even sympathetic measurement can kill. . . .)

Finally, a piece of blatant special pleading. I work in a former university extramural department. Extramural work has been going through a crisis of identity for some time, as more adults enter higher education and other advanced learning opportunities come on stream, notably via the web and other new technologies. In some cases such departments flourish with renewed vigour; elsewhere they have all but disappeared, or have been converted to units selling short courses to maximise university revenues. I believe that this tradition is ripe for revival and reinterpretation. The extramural function of the future is twofold. First, to enable citizens to come together, learn together and exchange views on issues of civic importance in a forum which is relatively protected from commercial interests. It is a crucial forum for the development of critical understanding in an age when flows of information are so heavily influenced by corporate interests. Secondly, a more active function is to promote the engagement of those learners in the myriads of civic organisations to whose activities the adult education programmes relate, from a local archaeological group to a campaign for global justice, putting this critical understanding to effective use. The acronymically challenged Higher Education Reach Out to Business and the Community (HEROBAC) initiative has got off to a quite promising start, with £60 million now committed in a regular funding stream. It needs to be consolidated, enlarged and—crucially—balanced in its two key terms, with community recognised as much as business. Above all, the links and partnerships which it rightly aims to foster should be given a broad and generous framework to work within, providing the institutional infrastructure and set of networks within which both human and social capital can accumulate.

We can construe the links between active citizenship and lifelong learning as two-way, symbiotic. They must span the economic and the civic spheres without subordination of one to the other. Where they flourish they will produce more argumentative, even awkward citizens, whose argumentativeness and awkwardness will be a mite better informed and significantly more empathetic.

Notes

1 Robert Putnam, *Bowling Alone: The Decline and Revival of Civic Engagement*, New York, Simon & Schuster, 2000.
2 Geraint Parry, George Moyser and Neil Day, *Political participation and democracy in Britain*, Cambridge, CUP, 1992.
3 See Michael Woolcook, 'Social capital and economic development: Towards a theoretical synthesis and policy framework', in *Theory and Society* 27, pp. 151–208; and Tom Schuller, Stephen Baron and John Field, 'Social Capital: A Review and Critique' in S. Baron, J. Field and T. Schuller, eds., *Social Capital: Critical Perspectives*. Oxford, OUP, 2000.
4 Michael Johnston and Roger Jowell, 'Social Capital and the Social Fabric' in R. Jowell et al., eds., *British Social Attitudes; 16th Report: Who Shares New Labour Values?*, Aldershot, Ashgate, 1999.
5 Peter Hall, 'Social Capital in Britain', in *British Journal of Political Science*, 29, 1999, pp. 417–61.
6 John Field and Tom Schuller, 'Networks, norms and trust: explaining patterns of lifelong learning in Scotland and Northern Ireland' in Frank Coffield, ed., *Differing visions of a Learning Society*, Cambridge, Polity Press, 2000.
7 O.E.C.D., *The Well-being of Nations: The role of human and social capital*, Paris, Organisation for Economic Cooperation and Development, 2001.
8 *Citizenship for 16–19 Year Olds in Education and Training*, Further Education Funding Council, 2000.
9 Nicholas Emler and Elizabeth Frazer, 'Politics: the education effect', in *Oxford Review of Education* 25, 1/2, pp. 251–73.

Relationships Between Work and Life

It is 10 years since Speaker Weatherill said, in explanation of the recommendations of his 1990 Commission for Citizenship, that people do not become good citizens by accident, any more than they become good nurses, good engineers, good bus drivers or computer scientists.[1] This chapter argues that people not only have to learn to be good citizens, but the structures have to be there for them to exercise citizenship rights and responsibilities actively and fully. This applies throughout life and through work as well as social and community life. Three commonly held misconceptions have impeded this:

(1) The view that citizenship is a status automatically acquired at the age of majority. People do not therefore have to learn it, or at best, need only preparatory education while at school.
(2) The view that the exercise of citizenship is an adjunct to the main business of earning a living.
(3) That most people still have standardised biographies, in which status as an adult citizen means being economically active for a period of forty years before retirement supported by benefits accrued during more or less continuous working life.

The idea that people gain and exercise rights and responsibilities sequentially and cumulatively is no longer the norm, any more than is the nuclear family. Changes in status are often provisional, sometimes reversible.

This chapter argues that, at the start of the new millennium, citizenship is more usefully seen as a *process* through which people exercise responsibility and social contribution while having entitlements to forms of social support which enable them to manage their own life and work situations and pursue their own projects. This approach to citizenship recognises that institutional and social structures constrain or empower people in the acquiring of the various forms of knowledge and competence necessary to independent existence and to the ability to make a contribution to society. In spanning the public and private domains of existence, it recognises social inequalities and inconsistencies of status at various stages in the course of life. Adults may, for example, be supporting a family while on a grant, or still in training. Or they may hold responsible positions in work while remaining in their family of origin, still the child in the household but supporting other members financially. In this way individual roles and status become differentiated across the different domains of life and experience, and so defining an individual as adult and citizen may hinge on the multiple roles performed. People may be caught in disjunctions and contradictions of policies which do not recognise the interplay of the private and public domains, policies often

© The Political Quarterly Publishing Co. Ltd. 2001

Published by Blackwell Publishers, 108 Cowley Road, Oxford OX4 1JF, UK and 350 Main Street, Malden, MA 02148, USA

based on invalid assumptions about common characteristics and the needs of different age ranges or social groups. To understand transitions to adult, worker and citizen status, we also have to understand the private world of family life.

In public policy debates about preparing people for the demands of 'adult and working life' the exercise of citizenship has tended to be treated as though it were an adjunct to the main business of working for a living. The rather lukewarm reception given to proposals to strengthen citizenship education in schools turns stone cold when the proposals start to extend beyond 16. Preparation for the 'real world' of employment starts to dominate. Yet, as Bernard Crick has argued,[2] preparation for citizenship clearly cannot end at age sixteen, at the very time when young people begin to have more access to the opportunities, rights and responsibilities of adult citizenship and the world of work. The need for an exploration of the ideas and practices of citizenship is evident whether young people are in education or in work-based training. I argue that this extends into and throughout adult life. These ideas are impeded by the concept of citizenship as a status acquired at a fixed point. They are facilitated when we approach citizenship as a lifelong process of engagement with the ideas and practices of democracy. How citizenship is conceptualised plays an important role in shaping perceptions and beliefs about the 'right' domains for the exercise of citizenship. I argue that citizenship, when viewed as a process, overarches work and economic contribution to society and encourages us to see workplace as important a context for the exercise of citizenship as community and neighbourhood.

Social Dynamics, Experience and Participation

Any analysis of how citizenship culture can be advanced has to take account of the changing nature of work and the effects on people's lives of the changing social landscape. What are conditions under which learning for adult life takes place? Which versions of citizenship are required? How can they best be achieved? In all European countries, young adults are experiencing uncertainty of status and are dependent upon state and parental support for longer periods than would have been the case a generation ago. Faced with changing structures of opportunity, people have to find their own ways of reconciling personal aspirations with available opportunities and their own values in the domains of education, consumption, politics, work and family life.

In the work arena, transitions to worker status are defined by institutionalised rules concerning recognised qualifications and credentials. The ways in which people negotiate systems of selection and accreditation are heavily influenced by cultural and social 'capital', the resources which come from family background and social networks and are important in providing access to information, advice, social, financial and career support. Adults bring different types of behaviour to the different situations of life. Success in negotiating these structures and networks can bring stability or instability to the whole course of people's lives. For those who are unsuccessful in gaining entry to jobs, long term unemployment cuts people off from the opportunities of the market, from access to work-based systems of gaining credentials and from the exercise of citizenship in any significant sense Even successful entry to the labour market can bring another set of limitations and instabilities. For beginning work too early can create premature foreclosure of options and fixed stereotypes of what kind of work is appropriate. In the 1950s workplaces were described in the Crowther Report (Ministry of Education 1959) as deadening to the minds of young school leavers. Lifelong learning policies of the year 2000 now talk of learning organisations. These are claimed to provide the model for the future, providing new opportunities for democratic access to knowledge. But only a small minority of enterprises match up to the model, while for those in the increasing ranks of casualised labour, training in narrowly-based competences is unlikely to be of any use over time. Members of casualised pools of labour are kept in on-going insecurity and instability, and so are unlikely to be able to engage in full participation in society in the sense implied in the maximal definitions of citizenship discussed earlier.

I also argue that citizenship rights should not become a *quid pro quo*, a social contract in which rights are tied to employment status. However, it can be argued that social rights should be re-examined in the light of increased demands for people to be 'flexible' and 'adaptable' in relation to the labour market, with the high insecurity that entails. When people become more flexible to employers' needs, this can often mean reduced scope for flexibility in other aspects of their lives. Therefore seeing citizenship as a process has implications for rights as well as responsibilities. Expanded social rights can include, for example, the right to choose more family friendly patterns of living and working and rights to paid educational leave. Expanding the conception of social rights in this way could go some way to stabilising our high insecurity society and countering some of its most damaging features, while providing a strengthened base for a citizen culture.

How have the changing situations of employment of the '80s and '90s affected people's attitudes to work? For some time, there was a version of 'moral panic' over the effects of unemployment on people's motivations to work. The traditional incentives of 'get good qualifications and get a good job' could not be invoked by teachers; and fears that a generation would be raised lacking the 'work-ethic' were pronounced in the early 1980s. The expansion of post-compulsory education has produced a new set of structures and experiences between the end of the compulsory phase of schooling at 16 and first entry to the labour market, at ages up to the mid-twenties. In England, the approach of 'vocationalism' has been to surround young people with a range of work-related opportunities for learning relatively early in their educational careers, but the opportunities for progressing from learning into work are haphazard and risky.[3] There is also an expectation of prolonged dependency associated with extended post-compulsory education, which runs counter to the deeply embedded cultural values and expectations of a significant proportion of the working class population, particularly among males. While access to education is a right of social citizenship, in the post-compulsory phase this has become associated with decreased social citizen-ship rights in other areas, associated with increased dependency and expectations of family support. In fact, the decline of employment opportun-ities 'tightened the bonds' between education and employment in a host of ways. High levels of work motivation and beliefs in personal responsibility for employment success were sustained, but the 'work ethic', with its connotations of social citizenship, has been replaced in large part by the 'consumer ethic', reflected in the common portrayal of citizenship rights as consumer rights.

Actual Citizenship Participation

While participation in work has been a preoccupation for policy makers, learning for citizenship must also relate to the ways in which people participate in their communities. As well as having rights and responsibilities as producers and consumers, they have rights and responsibilities to participate in the life of their local communities as citizens and voters. The democratic citizen is a politically informed and active citizen. How far do our adult populations in Europe meet these criteria? It is instructive to ask whether political engagement is increasing or decreasing in Europe? Is it confined to well-educated minorities? Eurobarometer surveys and the Euro-pean Values surveys indicate as a general trend in all countries an increase in political participation since the 1950s.[4] They also indicate that highly active forms of participation in politics are practised by a growing, but small, minority (increased from 4 to 10 per cent between 1974 and 1990) with some minor engagement in political activity increasing from 27 to 46 per cent over the same period in Europe as a whole; and when the figures are broken down by country, this trend towards higher levels of political activity is present in all countries.

The majority of European citizens now have some engagement and participation in political activity, with an overall increase from 31 per cent to 56 per cent. These figures include all forms of political participation, including a rise in direct action. Identification with political parties has grown in Greece, Portugal and Spain in contrast with the decline in Sweden, Ireland, Italy and France. The decline in Britain and West Germany of the 1970s has been reversed in the '80s and '90s. The Eurobarometer surveys show that 93 per cent of Western Europeans believed in the legitimacy of democracy as the way to govern, and a stable 50–60 per cent said that they were 'very satisfied' or 'fairly satisfied' with the way in which democracy operated in their own country between 1976 and 1991.

In Europe, general support for Western forms of democracy is stable and has continued at a high level. Governments often lose support, but active political engagement is generally low and lack of support for particular governments does not present a challenge to the general political system. In the post-communist states, however, the political culture (attitudes towards government and political authorities) necessary to a stability of the political system has been slow to develop. When access to hoped-for affluence is postponed, expectations are unfulfilled and disillusion sets in. There are differences between the post-communist world and western democracies in the importance attached to voluntary organisations and interest groups which reflect the degree of reliance of the former on state-directed strategies. Civil society—in the form of interest groups independent of the state—has considerable political potential. It has long been argued that, having groups able to organise themselves and act independently of the state is important for the viability of democracy, and the extent and form of interest group organisation within European countries is an important indicator of demo-cracy and stability. However, in a 'high insecurity' society, the self-protective features of interest groups may have increasingly negative implications for stability. Civil society without civic virtues may be dangerous for the future of democracy.

Surveys in post-communist states also show that parliamentary trust and confidence decreased in the mid-1990s. Despite this, political engagement in the form of subjective interest in politics and future voting intentions is comparable with levels in Western European countries and the principles of parliamentary democracy appear broadly accepted. These trends form the backcloth for research into the views, values and experiences of younger adults in changing socio-economic environments in Western Europe.

The effects of globalisation threaten to disassociate people from their traditional contexts. This means that in the search for identity or sense of wholeness and continuity as a person, all this gains a new intensity. Intergenerational transmission of 'virtues' is reduced, and the channels to participation in political and social structures may become obscured. Engage-ment in citizenship in its maximal sense is thus made more difficult, and the pursuit of 'ego-driven' projects may become paramount, as people act to maximise personal opportunity and reduce risk. Many of the 'choices' people exercise are rooted in partly-formed social identities, the senses people have of who they are and what their capabilities are. Self definition involves internalising the definitions and attributes ascribed by others. These sub-jective identities are associated with social class, gender and ethnicity. They also reflect the educational credentials gained and other mediating factors associated with experiences in the labour market and in wider social contexts. Disadvantage continues to be concentrated in groups defined by class, gender and ethnicity in particular localities. Social identities are reflected in social attitudes. Post-school learning environments may be pivotal for future patterns of learning, social participation and the exercise of citizenship in later adult life, yet most attention, in the European context, is given to preparation for work and careers. Changes in political involvements between

16 and 20 are incremental, with only a tiny minority developing any serious involvement in politics of the conventional kind.[5] Their attitudes are not organised around political positions but around the politics of the personal. Changes in early adult life involved gradual increases in interest in political issues.

How Active Are Young People?

Do we know to what extent 18–25 year olds are active agents in their lives outside work? How does this compare with their agency inside work and their work values? The Economic and Social Research Council project 'Taking Control: agency in young adult transitions in England and the New Germany' is investigating these questions by comparing the values and experiences of young adults in the three cities of Derby, Hannover and Leipzig. Charts 1 and 2 compare research participants' mean scores on indices of career-seeking behaviour and politically active group behaviour. These findings suggest that individualised market oriented behaviours appear most strongly in the setting in which markets have been deregulated and individualised behaviours have been most strongly encouraged or enforced—that of the English labour market. In all groups the German respondents, both from the West and the *Länder* of the East were less proactive in relation to the labour market (e.g. in job-seeking) than their English counterparts. They also showed more politically active group behaviour in the form of participation in political events and engagement in political discussions.

The juxtaposition of these two findings suggests that concerns about the erosion of citizenship in consumer and market driven socio-economic environments may be well founded. This is underlined when voting intentions and levels of political interest declared by respondents are examined. Answers to the 'would you vote . . . ?' question suggest quite an important international difference. 73 per cent in the East German sample and 78 per cent in the West German sample said 'yes', compared to a considerably lower 61 per cent in England. There were also important differences between groups, with more in the unemployed groups stating that they would not vote.

This was not just apathy on the part of English respondents, because 37 per cent did answer the question, but said 'no' positively, they wouldn't vote. There were also important differences between groups, with more in the unemployed groups stating that they would not vote. They seem to be making a conscious decision *not* to do something. Are the German political parties better at appealing to or representing this age group? The German interviews do suggest a stronger interest and critical engagement in formal politics and political issues than is found in the English groups, although both are highly critical of politics and politicians. It should also be noted that in all groups political activity and interest increases with age, a finding which reinforces those of previous studies and confirms that this is not a phenomenon of young Germans retaining 'student' identities longer in the more

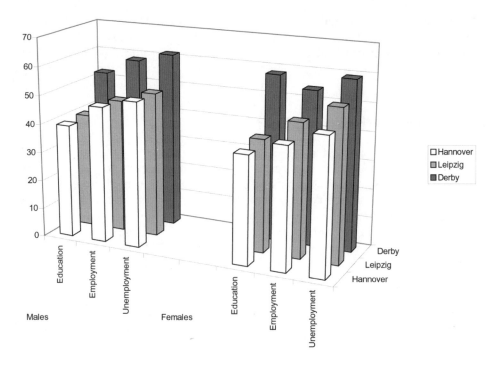

Chart 1: Career-seeking behaviour (N=900, n=100 in each setting in each city)

highly institutionalised German environment. There were important differences when different types of activity or behaviour were examined. Involvement in political organisations was also compared with involvement in religious and sports organisations and for relative importance with other aspects of personal and social life.

Table 1 gives percentages of respondents (n=300 in each city) who have engaged in the listed activity once or more. Activities 2 and 3, where the English outscore the Germans are 'individual' political acts, the other items are arguably more social/communal. The behaviour among English 18–25 year olds did not reflect a high degree of collective agency. The German/English difference on item 5 is noticeable, but not large. It is possible that more politics/citizenship education in schools and in post-school learning environments in England could lead to an increase here. The difference in Item 1 also suggests more overt political activity on the part of the German respondents. Are the Germans more comfortable with day-to-day, personal political interactions? Does their cultural context encourage this? The low numbers joining political organisations can be contrasted with the high levels of affiliation to sports organisations and the proportions who join religious organisations. (The high figure for religious affiliations in Hannover is typical for the area.)

Turning to the group interview transcripts, the following extracts typify the

© The Political Quarterly Publishing Co. Ltd. 2001

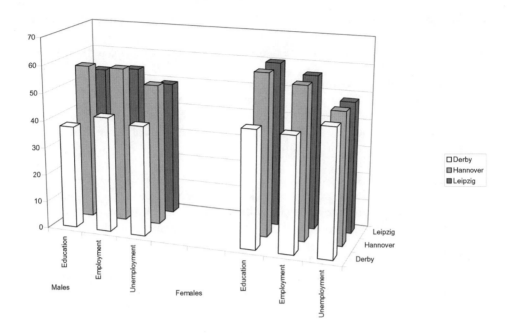

Chart 2: Politically active group behaviour (N=900, n=100 in each setting in each city)

Table 1: Participation in activities and organisations

	Derby	Leipzig	Hannover
1. Attended a political meeting/rally	32	71	72
2. Given views to a politician	21	17	16
3. Handed out leaflets	25	9	11
4. Helped organise public meetings	32	37	47
5. Discussed political views with family/friends	74	90	91
6. Joined a trade union	16	15	13
7. Joined a political party	1	4	8
8. Joined a religious organisation	23	21	58
9. Joined a sports organisation	74	60	62

range of German and English comments on politics. They reflect a mix of passive, resigned and resistant and proactive stances:

Derby Higher Education Group
M: It's hard for us to be interested really. I mean Labour got in and one of the first things they did was to cut student grants, wasn't it? So we can't really be happy about that.

C: We were all rooting for them and then they did that, and now it's like 'go away!'

M: That's right. I think, well, I just can't be bothered anymore with any of it.

Hannover Employed Group

A: I do not know a thing about politics. I am not interested in it very much.

B: We cannot influence them anyway. Once they are the leaders they want to lead all alone. I believe that there is no use getting involved in it at all, that is, that there is anything I can do about it.

Leipzig Employed Group

K: I am not interested in politics, you know. These people who rule are of no use anyway. I can vote for a party but nothing will improve. I am fed up with politics when I look at the situation on the apprenticeship market.

Derby Higher Education Group

A: I do think it is important to some extent to understand the politics that affect you, not necessarily politics full stop. But, I'm not very up to date with it all myself.

Derby Employment Group

D: Politics, I think is quite important with the job I do, because with the benefits system, if they change it, I've got to be up to date on it because of the advice that I give people and if I give them the wrong advice then . . . . But I don't really care for it myself. It's only when it's relevant to my job that I take any notice.

Hannover Higher Education Group

A: You are not serious, asking me this question are you? Of course, to me politics is very important, very very important.

Hannover Unemployment Group

C: I think politics is very important. Politics creates the framework for our lives. It influences our lives in all spheres, work but also leisure too.

Leipzig Higher Education Group

T: Politics begins in your residential district. There you can change something. Big politics however. . . .

K: Sure you can. For example, by organising a demo.

The strongest expressions of political activism came from a minority in the German groups. Interest in the Derby group appeared to be more motivated by individual self-interest. But many in both countries take a negative view, along the lines of 'they're all the same', 'you can't change anything'. 'All the things they tell you at election time sound so good but when the election is over they do not remember what they promised to the people. I do not think that I can influence politics.' Although the English were often negative it could be argued that this is more a case of rejection than apathy; they have usually 'made a choice' to be negative which again suggests that the English parties have done too little to appeal to this age group.

Work Values and Activities Outside Work

The research also examined how far scope for responsibility and achievement were emphasised in work values, when considered alongside features such as wages, job security, atmosphere and collective contribution. The chart for the groups in employment settings is given below. The charts broadly followed similar patterns in the Higher Education and employment groups, the most important differences being the national ones.

In all settings, job security continues to be highly valued by the German respondents. A good salary or wage is most highly valued by the English, but less so by the German respondents. 'Affiliation' factors to do with the people you meet and work with are important for a friendly atmosphere, but not for relationships. Collective and 'service to society' values were

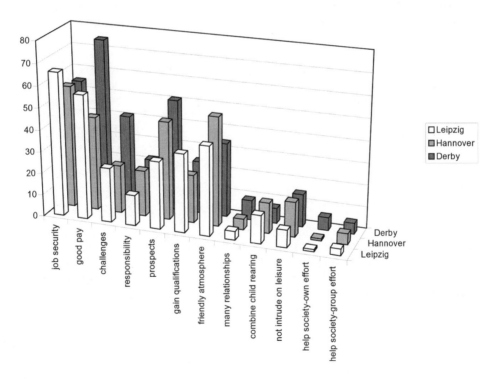

Chart 3: Work values in employment (N=900, n=100 in each setting in each city)

rated as important by only a few respondents in each setting and area. The previous socialisation of the Leipzig group into collective values and the subordination of the individual to the collective good has disappeared in the values expressed in this survey.

In 1997, in the second survey of the DJI (German Youth Institute),[6] 7,000 young people in East and West Germany were asked about their relationship towards politics. The findings of that study are consistent with the author's present study. Work and profession are still central elements in the life plans of younger people. 'The risks of unemployment and uncertainties in professional biographies seem dangerous to them.' The first demand German young adults place on politics is to secure and enlarge opportunities for qualifications and workplaces that promise well for their future. 'Work shall be more than earning money and citizenship more than voting' for German youth. The ideal of democracy is estimated highly including participation in school, university and in public in general. The study showed, however, that there was dissatisfaction with the 'realities' of the state, the parties and politicians and little confidence in the institutions.

In the *Länder* of the former DDR the majority are critical of the political realities of the Federal Republic. The gap between the support of the idea of democracy and the satisfaction with the democratic everyday reality is marked in the new Länder and consistent with the wider trends in post-communist societies. It has been suggested that the feelings of young East Germans reflect their belief that they are disadvantaged because they do not get their just share of the wealth—'the subjective balance sheets turns out to be more often negative for the East Germans'. Findings show that Eastern German respondents do not believe that there are equal opportunities for all, while more of their Western German counterparts do believe this. East Germans perceive the influences of structurally based 'acquired' attributes to be more important in affecting people's opportunities in life than their West German counterparts, while English respondents perceive these influences as least important.[7]

Government Influence

In England, government policy emphasises the need for a strong civil society combined with citizenship, and the question of citizenship education in Further and Adult Education is being newly addressed. This needs to recognise that interest in politics increases with age, and to understand better the ways in which biographical events occur which make civic and political engagement more immediately relevant. In Germany, where citizenship and values education has been enshrined in the curriculum not only at school, but also in the *Berufsschulen*, the citizenship education debate has been centred on the 'integration' of the new *Länder* after the political upheavals and on the appropriate aims of citizenship education after 16. Questions of nationality and access to citizenship rights have also dominated the national agenda; with obvious implications for citizenship education. In Eastern Germany, expectations of state-driven responses to social issues appear to remain quite high. For adult educators, the transformation process of adult education in the new federal states was presented as an opportunity to reconsider positions and prejudices. In practice, the market forces which swept a wave of new market providers into the new states, deepened the mistrust of citizens in the new system.[8]

The views, values and experiences of people differ according to their position in the social landscape; the various settings of education, unemployment and employment are marked in all three cities and most recognise structural constraints on action. Citizenship education has high potential to engage with the multi-dimensional nature of people's lives, and to recognise the extent to which agency can be exercised outside formal structures. Disengagement from collective activities of all kinds is, however, as marked as the apparent strength of individual agency. The lack of connection into democratic structures in communities and workplaces appears to be the most pressing problem to be addressed.

The metaphor for human agency which sees people as 'actors in the social landscape' carries implications for the actual citizenship curriculum. For this must relate, at any age or stage, to a framework for interpreting the world as a social whole, while understanding the sources of diversity and differentiation within it. A strengthened citizen culture needs people to learn about, for and through citizenship. For adults this requires:

- moving beyond policy preoccupations with key skills and narrow forms of competence, towards the development of what I have termed 'educated attributes'—the combination in adult life of values, knowledge skills and

Bringing the elements together

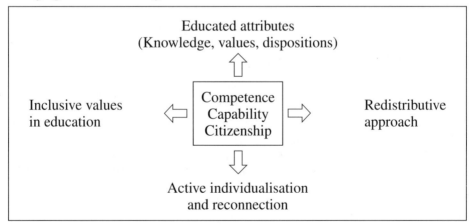

Figure 1: Education for citizenship

dispositions also requires approaches which are both inclusive *and* redistributive;[9]

- connection into democratic structures where skills and dispositions of active citizenship can be exercised. Where are these structures for those moving through and out of various forms of post-school education and training and trying to gain a foothold in the institutions of work and adult life? Where are they for those adults in insecure positions and caught in the revolving doors of the labour market?

In local communities, democratic structures are there but are often not representative and do not attract broad based community involvement and engagement. Industrial democratic institutions such as works councils are generally not a feature of UK companies, and the employee voice is most often confined to weak forms of 'consultation' (in marked contrast to Works Councils in Germany). And effective consultation is further weakened by conditions of globalisation and the incorporation of 'employee voice' into the dominant corporate cultures of multi-national companies. All this adds to a conception that citizenship, if exercised at all in its critical and active sense, is something that is exercised outside workplaces.

This is part of the challenge: has democracy in the workplace reached a dead end? The point of production is not the prime locus of democratisation, but 'receptors' exist within the workplace domains for challenges to anti-democratic practices.[10] The potential is there to expand in a democratic way structures for discussion and compromise: projects of democratic institutional reform can be realistically aimed at

- broadening and democratising the structures of discussion and compromise which already exist
- enabling the exercise of expanded forms of social rights, through negotiation and agreement
- enabling bodies representative of workers to play expanded roles in, for example, development of collective frameworks for learning and employee development. If citizenship is a process then strengthened provision and entitlements for paid educational leave at all ages are needed.

The exercise of citizenship as a process, in relation to changing structures of work and community, requires a more highly mobilised civil society, accompanied by 'civic virtues' and structures for democratic participation. This can be an 'upward spiral' process with increased democratisation of structures strengthening civic virtues, expectations of participation and political knowledge. Conversely, participation through education and lifelong learning will challenge anti-democratic practices and strengthen civil society. We have also to be alert to the possibility that the spiral can work in a downwards direction, with erosion of citizenship.

My argument basically reflects a neo-republican viewpoint. It voices concern about low engagements in politics and it advocates support for community education to stimulate political participation and support for direct democracy through creation of structures such as neighbourhood associations and modern versions of workplace councils. It also recognises that people learn to participate first in the collective 'free spaces' of life, and argues that the non-commercialised free spaces of collective life have to be both protected and expanded. Minimally they have to be protected from further erosion. Citizenship means engagement in both institutionalised and informal discourse. At the level of the individual citizen, it involves a complex interplay of rationality and subjectivity. Reconciliation between rationality and subjectivity comes when social actors can play a part in shaping their social environments. This means not only the competence to 'read the world' and reflect critically on it,[11] but also the disposition to be active in the world. Creation and recreation of the democratic structures which allow the disposition to act to be translated into effective action are essential to the safeguarding of democracy. This is a radical perspective which envisages sustained educational engagement with the social reality of people's lives as actors in the social landscape of society and in their communities. It challenges dominant assumptions about 'front-end' schooling. It also has implications for the form and content of that educational engagement.

The upsurge of interest in lifelong-learning could, with political will behind it, accelerate the development of expanded approaches to citizenship education; but the latter requires much more emphasis on citizenship as a process. It also needs to recognise that citizenship is actually a larger category than work in people's lives. Citizenship is a lifelong process, which links rather than separates generations. It incorporates working lives: it is not simply an adjunct to the business of working for a living. It requires not only larger and more generous understandings of what constitutes learning about, for and by citizenship; it also depends on strengthening the support and development of the democratic structures and viable means of social/ educational redistribution which can make the real exercise of citizenship possible for all.

Acknowledgement

The author gratefully acknowledges the support of the UK Economic and Social Research Council, in the form of Award No L134 251 011 in the Youth Citizenship and Social Change Programme: 'Taking Control': Agency in Young Adult Transitions in England and new Germany. Thanks are also due to my co-researchers, Martina Behrens, Jens Kaluza, Peter Rudd, Claire Woolley for their contributions to the wider study, and to John Dobby, previously senior statistician at NFER.

Notes

1 B. Weatherill, *Speaker's Commission. Encouraging Citizenship*, London, HMSO, 1990
2 See also the 1999 DfEE Report, 'Preparing Young People for Adult Life'.

3 K. Evans and W. Heinz, *Becoming Adults in England and Germany*, London, Anglo-German Foundation, 1994.
4 Eurobarometer surveys 6–35, Brussels, European Commission.
5 M. Banks et al, *Careers and Identities*, Buckingham, Open University Press, 1992.
6 M. Gille and W. Kruger, DJl Jugensurvey 2, Leske and Budrich, 2000.
7 K. Evans et al, 'Reconstructing Fate as Choice', Nordic Youth Research International Symposium Helsinki 2000; in press for journal YOUNG 2001/2.
8 M. Sporing, 'German Adult Education in East Germany after Unification: picking up the pieces, SCUTREA Proceedings, University of Southampton, 1995.
9 K. Evans, *Shaping Futures: Learning for Competence and Citizenship*, London, Macmillan 2000; K. Evans et al, *Learning and Work in the Risk Society*, London, Macmillan, 2000.
10 See Cohen and Arato, *Civil Society and Political Theory*, Cambridge, Mass., MIT Press, 1992.
11 M. Welton, M. Kamp and L. Veendrick, in D. Wildemeersch, M. Finger and T. Jansen, eds., *Adult Education and Social Responsibility*, Frankfurt am Main, Peter Lang, 2000.

The Voluntary Sector

ISOBEL LINDSAY

We have to . . . increase as far as possible the spaces and resources which enable alternative socialities to be produced, which allow modes of life, co-operation and activities to emerge that lie outside the power apparatuses of capital and the state. In other words, we have to maximise the number of paths 'out of capitalism'.[1]

THE past two decades have seen a growth of interest in the voluntary sector and in the idea of citizenship. Both are clearly inter-connected. The most obvious connection is around the volunteering element of the sector and the image of 'active citizenship'. But the connections are more complex than this and relate to ideas of political, social and economic pluralism and the development of varied 'points of initiative' in society.

It is not coincidental that interest in the sector has grown at the same time as the big ideological shifts around socialism and free-market capitalism. But it is an interest which comes from different ideological positions. Sections of the Right in the UK and the US are attracted to the voluntary sector model as an alternative to state provision of services when the private sector is not an option. This is essentially a reversion to the pre-Welfare State position. Of more interest has been the increased focus on the voluntary sector by sections of the Left. There are a number of more complex strands in this. These range from the straightforward pragmatic approach; where there is a social need which should be met and is not being met by the public sector, then it should be done by any other means possible. But there is also the more visionary 'big picture' approach; the expansion of the not-for-profit sector offers alternatives to the dominant for-profit model and it also presents an alternative pattern of political action through mobilisation by campaigning groups. The concept of the 'social economy' is increasingly being used, although precise definitions are difficult. So there is a significant intellectual and action agenda around the voluntary sector which has lots of scope for development in the coming decades.

There is also an explicitly political dimension. The voluntary sector has played an increasing role in brokering policies and establishing issues. For many major policy areas—international aid, the environment, poverty, discrimination—it is far more likely that it will be the campaigning organisations, not the political parties, which will have brought together people with shared interests, developed public opinion, and promoted reform programmes with public authorities. Political parties, beneath national leadership levels, have become election organisers with only a very marginal role in policy development. When virtually any major policy issues arise, there are active campaigning groups submitting recommendations, lobbying, leading comment in the media. This political role has arisen partly to fill the

© The Political Quarterly Publishing Co. Ltd. 2001
Published by Blackwell Publishers, 108 Cowley Road, Oxford OX4 1JF, UK and 350 Main Street, Malden, MA 02148, USA

vacuum created by the diminution of the party political role; but it has also evolved because many issues have not fitted easily into the traditional political spectrum e.g. the environment or animal welfare.

This 'political' voluntary sector role has enabled a much wider participation in the political process to take place than through the party system. The citizen interested in public affairs may choose to pursue this in many different forms. In Scotland alone, there are around 44,000 voluntary organisations.[2] Anyone concerned with health issues might be a member of a small support group for those with a particular illness, might raise funds for one of the large research charities, might assist a health promotion campaign against smoking, might be a member of a lobbying organisation pressurising the Government to invest more in the health service. There has been a major expansion in the channels through which we can participate and it is questionable whether political institutions have adjusted sufficiently to this although the new devolved bodies may be more responsive.

Social Capital

The growth of the academic interest in 'social capital' has paralleled this growth in voluntary organisations. The idea of treating traditions of civic involvement and social solidarity as a form of capital, a store of valuables which can be used to generate further desirable outcomes for a society, became a popular theme in the 1990s, evolving from earlier work on civic cultures. It owes much to the work of Robert Putnam and his study of the relationship between economic success, effective government and civic participation in Italy.[3] Putnam examined the distribution of participation in local associations, local newspaper readership, and turnout in referendums. A clear correlation emerged between economic success and levels of civic participation (apart from church membership) and Putnam suggested that the direction of causation was mainly from the civic participation to the economic/political success. In the most civic regions, such as Emilia-Romagna, citizens are actively involved in a wide variety of groups—local bands, sports clubs, literary guilds, co-operatives. There is a high readership of local newspapers and extensive conviction politics. In the least civic regions like Calabria, there is a low level of local clubs and media and a preponderance of hierarchical patron/client networks. Group membership is twice as high in Emilia-Romagna as in Calabria. Organised group participation, it is suggested, encourages negotiating skills, initiative, trust, a perception of the broader public interest. Participation does not necessarily reduce conflicts but it does give people social tools to negotiate conflicts.

If there are grounds for accepting even part of this analysis, it does suggest that encouraging civic involvement is advantageous for stimulating many kinds of spin-offs and that once a culture of involvement is established, it is potentially self-perpetuating although this is by no means automatic. Putnam in his latest book[4] sees a reversal in social behaviour in the US away from the now elderly 'civic generation' towards the more individualistic.

Tensions in the Sector

There are, however, difficult tensions in the voluntary sector that are likely to increase. Currently the sector has two major roles. There is a growing role being promoted by both Labour and Conservatives for service delivery by voluntary organisations rather than by the public sector. The outcome of this has been and may increasingly be that a major part of the sector becomes dependent on state contracts with a status in some respects like quangos but with less security. Organisations are competing against each other in a short-term contract culture. There is an established record in many organisations for good quality and participative service delivery. There is considerable potential to expand this; but there are also elephant traps along the way. The sector might end up being used as a cheap option with an insecure and fragmented labour force or they might find themselves responsible for a substantial increase in service delivery which requires them to become too large and highly bureaucratised, in the process losing some of those valuable qualities of responsiveness and participation which have characterised the best of services.

The other role is that of the sector as a major component of the 'opposition' to whatever government is in power, the channel for those pursuing social change either through campaigning, advocacy or transformative action programmes. They may not be hostile to governments but they are going to challenge on a permanent basis. This role involves problems of funding sources which can be accessed without unduly compromising the position of critic. The reality on the ground is that many organisations encompass both roles. In addition there are significant issues which arise with the growing professionalism in organisations and the tension between this and lay participation. So the future direction of the sector and its relationship to a culture of citizenship has potential but also problems. It can be the central resource for the development of active citizenship or it can become just another set of employers who cannot maintain an independent role because of their financial relationships with the private or public sectors. An awareness of these problems should help us develop what is best in the sector.

The Social Economy

There is a growing interest in the idea of the social economy. To some extent this is presentational, changing the way much of the work of the sector is perceived. But it has the potential to be more than this—to offer an example of those 'routes out of capitalism' to which Andre Gorz referred. Although the term 'social economy' is now widely used in the European and UK context, there is no clear agreement on definition. In the UK the conventional definition of the social economy has focused on local job-creation projects providing local services with volunteer leadership. However a broader definition is merited. Those services and goods which are provided by public benefit associations—that is organisations pursuing a broadly defined public benefit on a non-profit distributing basis, these should come into the social economy category. This encourages us to focus on the meaning of economic in a context which is not dominated by monetarised values.

Recreation for disabled children, lunch clubs for the elderly, conservation projects, sports clubs, credit unions—these can all be seen in conventional economic language as providing added value for the community in general or specific groups within it. Some of these services may have costs attached to them for consumers, for example charity shops. Some will give not sell services. But this is as much economic activity as is commercial trading. If a charity shop is operated on behalf of a health charity, it performs a useful recycling function for goods which would otherwise involve a disposal cost for the community. It provides low-cost goods for those who need them. It is likely to provide paid employment at some point in the managerial chain. It will contribute through income generated to the employment of highly-skilled professionals in medical care or research. This is a small example of the economic role of activities still frequently viewed as marginal or dis-counted in the context of conventional economic policy-making.

The social economy usually has to be highly entrepreneurial. Much of the work involves start-ups and there are few standard, traditional jobs. They have to use entrepreneurial skills to put together funding packages from diverse public grants, charitable income and revenue streams from services. They are job-creating. Currently voluntary organisations in Scotland employ 3 per cent of the labour force and direct a substantial additional amount of unpaid labour in the form of 700,000 volunteers. What can this social economy contribute? Many of the social groups or geographical areas in which organisations operate are unattractive to the private sector because they are low-income. Credit unions are an example of financial service provision among groups for whom commercial banks do not wish to cater because they do not generate sufficient profit. Social economy organisations not only contribute services or goods, they are a valuable source of formal and informal training.

There is also work that can be done more effectively than conventional public sector provision. It can often provide better local involvement. Participants are likely to be more local to an area than, say, officials of the local authority or the Employment Service. There is more flexibility, with local management committees able to take part in lobbying and campaigning as well as service delivery. However, although much of what has been perceived as the social economy in the narrow definition has been situated in the local and among the poor, this is too limited a perspective. Environmental or cultural groups, for example, may operate in areas that are comparatively prosperous and they may contribute to the prosperity of the area through the impact on the tourist industry as well as being a valued service in themselves. Local initiatives are frequently part of national organisational structures which co-ordinate a range of programmes, such as Citizens' Advice Bureaux, Barnardo's etc.. And there are services whose direction may be mainly national such as the National Trust for Scotland.

If we focus on the value of the work rather than on perceptions of what is economic based on narrow commercial definitions, we see both the potential for expansion of the non-commercial sector and the opportunity for participation in work as citizens in a wide variety of contexts. We may work full-time or part-time, paid or as volunteers in varying combinations in different stages of our lives. Also there is an important area of economic activity to which we can contribute in organisations run for 'public benefit' and which seek to generate or reinforce the notion of a responsibility to the community.

If we are to expand this social economy, we do need to address some policy issues. The Kemp Report[5] argued for the need to redefine charitable status and create the new category of public benefit associations. There is an urgent need for the law around mutual associations to be reviewed. We need recognition of the role of social economy organisations so that they can gain access to some of the support available to for-profit companies from development agencies. We are seeing some movement in the latter with Highlands and Islands Enterprise having led the way[6] and Scottish Enterprise beginning to show some interest. We need investment in training volunteers in general management and social entrepreneurial skills. Above all we need to be imaginative in how we expand and give status to this not-for-profit sector.

Voluntary, Public and Private: Maintaining Independence

One of the problems identified as growing in importance is that of keeping the independence of the sector. Voluntary organisations are a vital part of the democratic process. They have the responsibility of representing the interests and objectives of a large section of the public. They need to be trusted to promote these even if it results in offending those in positions of power. If they lose this trust, they will be regarded with the same cynicism that many feel, rightly or wrongly, for political parties. They also have to judge how close to get to decision-makers. It may help in gaining their objectives or it may blunt the edge of their role as critic and compromise them. The latter is one of the eternal problems of politics which depends on case by case judgement but the issues around financial dependency are widespread and growing in importance. These require more consideration.

The voluntary sector is faced with increased problems of funding which may place stresses on its independence. Most organisations are under pressure to become increasingly 'professional' in their approach. Even applications for a modest amount of funding from any source are likely to involve the production of business plans, accounts, performance records, mission statements. This creates more demand for trained staff that requires either employing them or spending money training volunteers. Fund-raising from the general public has become much more sophisticated and expensive as organisations find they have to compete in the context of commercial media promotion. This does not come cheap but not to invest in promotion may mean declining donated income.

There is also the imbalance between core and project funding. The former is a less attractive proposition since it involves no innovation or clear outputs. Project funding, on the other hand, is more attractive and the sources of project funding have probably increased. Funders want to back new developments but many organisations as a result find themselves caught on a treadmill. To keep core organisational work going, they need constantly to develop new projects. This in turn puts increased stress on their core structures. Public authorities are a major source of core funding as well as project funding. Many organisations are very conscious of their vulnerability in this patron/client relationship. One example of this was the implied threat that homeless charities which did not go along with the Government's anti-begging message might be cut out of programmes.

Charitable trusts are another significant source of funding and have the advantage of having varied interests and perspectives but they can only perform a modest role. Private sector charitable giving has its place but can produce many ethical problems, especially where sponsorship or product promotion is involved.

The impact of the Lottery has been mixed. On the one hand it has been another source of funding, one step removed from Government. On the other hand, the evidence suggests that it has had a negative effect on direct public charitable donations. The omens are now even worse. The New Opportunities Fund which will now channel part of the Lottery funding has ceased even to put up much pretence about 'additionality'. It is going to fund projects which are, in effect, mainstream education and health service work. The temptation is very great for Governments to finance more of their service delivery through the N.O.F., with a diminishing amount going to the voluntary sector through the Lottery Charities Board. There are no easy answers to these funding problems but some new thinking is needed to try to address them for the sake of the independence and viability of the sector. One promising initiative would be to have a small addition to local and central taxation which taxpayers would have to opt out of if they did not wish to contribute. This would go into funding trusts for voluntary organisations to be administered not by government or 'the great and the good' but by some form of selection similar to jury service. Another route would be the more vigorous promotion of give as you earn workplace-based fund-raising. Also since the Lottery appears to be here to stay, the least Government could do would be to ring-fence more of it for voluntary sector finance rather than to act as an alternative funding source for public sector services.

One factor which is crucial to all of these independence questions is that the sector itself should become increasingly well-organised to create some 'strength in numbers'. Building up infrastructure, either on a geographical or interest basis, gives organisations greater bargaining power and a stronger public voice. The growth of 'umbrella' organisations has been a marked feature in recent years and this trend is likely to increase despite the fact that there have some failures. It might be seen by some as excessive bureau-cratisation but the advantages can be significant. Not the least of these is that local and central government, public boards or private companies will not face a large number of individual organisations when negotiating/consulting on issues but will have to deal with co-ordinated groups seeking to speak on some issues with one voice. Much of the time this suits state agencies since it is much easier to deal with a single organisation rather than a large number of individual groups. But it is also a source of protection. There are a range of Government programmes, especially around social inclusion, which depend on the voluntary sector for much of their delivery. If it was felt that the sector or sections of it were being unfairly treated, the capacity to act together and prevent 'divide and rule' could be effective.

Developing the Policy Role

One of the most important contributions the voluntary sector can make is in the field of policy development. Many organisations have built up two types of expertise. One type comes from experience in service provision. If you have provided services for the mentally ill, for refugees, for ex-prisoners, for lone parents, you are likely to have built up a considerable body of case material about what does and does not work and where the problems are in the system. The other type involves the collating and dissemination of a variety of research material. But how does this get into the policy process? Probably inconsistently. The traditional formal consultation process is deeply flawed. Organisations are asked for written comments on proposals which are unlikely to be greatly changed and they are often given a very short period to submit responses. Some who have adequate professional staff may be geared up to do this, others may find it difficult.

What is most needed is to develop input at an earlier and at a later stage in the process. The earlier stage which may be either with political parties or with central or local governments is when policy decisions are still fluid and genuinely open to influence. The later stage is that of assessing the effect of policy change among those most affected. Some of this happens now but we need to ensure that it is grounded in the system and that the nature of the input involves dialogue.

The parliamentary committee system, especially as it is developing in the new devolved assemblies, provides one route. The Civic Forum models in Northern Ireland, Scotland, London and possibly at a later stage in Wales, are another potentially very important development (about which I have written elsewhere).[7] These have the advantage that they provide an opportunity for dialogue across different areas of interest and enable civic organisations to raise and develop ideas which they feel are not being addressed by those in positions of power in public or private sectors.

Some of these roles which we now look to civic organisations to fill, might have been expected in the past to be carried out by political parties. Parties in the future may change and become more open arenas of policy debate but the signs are not encouraging. The voluntary/civic sector is now well-placed to provide that exploratory space for new thinking and to offer open access for any citizen to participate. What we need to do for the future is to build the institutional structures that will facilitate this role and build bridges between the concerned citizen, the activist and the politician.

Notes

1 Andre Gorz, *Reclaiming Work*, Cambridge, Polity Press, 1999.
2 *The Scottish Voluntary Sector Almanac, SCVO 1996. The UK Voluntary Sector Almanac*, NCVO 1966.
3 Robert Putnam, *Making Democracy Work, Princeton*, Princeton University Press, 1994.
4 Robert Putnam, *Bowling Alone: The Collapse and Revival of American Community*, New York, Simon & Schuster, 2000.
5 *Head and Heart: the report of the Commission on the Future of the Voluntary Sector In Scotland*, SCVO, 1997.
6 *An Assessment of the Social Economy in the Highlands and Islands*, ERM 1996.
7 Isobel Lindsay 'The New Civic Forums' *The Political Quarterly*, October–December 2000.

The Community Roots of Citizenship

HENRY TAM

CITIZENSHIP grows out of community life. Respect for each others' rights, and commitments to fulfilling one's responsibilities only move from the realm of abstract ideas to actual expressions when they are embedded in human interactions. When people no longer share a strong enough sense of common purpose, civic virtues fade. The decline in electoral turnout, the mantra for tax cuts, and the growing distrust of politicians are all symptoms of individuals becoming ill at ease in their role as citizens. Instead of making better use of the democratic tools of public policies and services, they prefer to retreat into their consumerist haven, where they can make their own choices, regardless of the implications for society at large.

No market-obsessed individualism can ever escape from a flawed view of citizens as consumers—entailing the deficient conception of public service as parasitic on the private pursuit of wealth and self-gratification. In reality, services which bind and sustain the public domain are the core elements of any civilised society. Those who dedicate themselves to serving the public good—be they elected or appointed, part-time or full-time, paid or volunteers—they are the ones who provide the foundations for citizenship, making it possible for 'less public spirited' individuals, so to speak, to pursue their own ends.

In large complex societies, all too many people, especially amongst the political elites, have long lost sight of this. They think wealth-generators are everything, and citizenship is about facilitating this wealth creation process. If a vibrant citizen culture is to be our objective, we must disabuse those soaked in plutocratic prejudices and reconnect our public services with civic pride. To do so, we need to help those concerned with the public good at the community level—local authorities, community groups, etc.—grow in confidence and flourish through the participation of local people. As John Stuart Mill, the outstanding philosopher-civil servant, explained in his *Considerations on Representative Government:* 'The maximum of the invigorating effect of freedom upon the character is only obtained when the person acted on either is, or is looking forward to becoming, a citizen as fully privileged as any other. What is still more important than even this matter of feeling is the practical discipline which the character obtains from the occasional demand made upon citizens to exercise, for a time and in their turn, some social function. . . . He is called upon, while so engaged, to weigh interests not his own; to be guided, in case of conflicting claims, by another rule than his private partialities; to apply, at every turn, principles and maxims which have for their reason of existence the common good: and he usually finds associated with him in the same work minds more familiarised than his own with these ideas and operations, whose study it will be to supply reasons to his understanding, and stimulation to his feeling for the general interest.' Furthermore, as Mill went on to say, '. . . I have dwelt . . . on the importance of that portion of the operation of free institutions which may be called the public education of the citizens. Now, of this operation the local administrative institutions are the chief instrument.'

The Decline of Local Democracy

In the UK, however, we have witnessed a significant decline in the role and functions of local public bodies for over half a century. First, the post-war Labour Government embarked upon a vast centralisation programme to create new national public services such as the National Health Service and different public utilities. Then the Conservatives further weakened local democracy by either transferring more local functions to the centre or shifting them out to the private sector altogether. In parallel with these developments, the ability of local government to raise its own tax revenue to meet local needs was radically curtailed. Citizens who once could have become involved with local institutions which impact on nearly all the key issues concerning their shared communities, now find that they can have little influence on corresponding bodies the performance targets and budgets of which are largely set by central bureaucracies remote from their lives. It is not surprising that their interest in selecting representatives to serve on such bodies, let alone participating directly themselves, has consistently diminished.

Whatever the rhetoric across the political spectrum may be regarding the promotion of active citizenship, recent trends have not been helpful. Regional development agencies have been created to take charge of economic strategies even though they will be run by a small board dominated by business people appointed by central government. In the name of service efficiency, the housing benefits administered by democratically elected local authorities will be integrated into a unified Benefits service (called 'One') along with the works of bodies with no local democratic accountabilities such as the Benefits Agency and the Employment Service. The well meaning 'Modernising Government' initiative to join up disparate public services is leading to the blurring of responsibilities and generating even more confusion in the public mind about who is accountable for what. The push for mayoral politics pins its hope on personality-driven publicity to raise electoral turnouts, whilst it ignores the fact that the concentration of power in a single individual not only increases the prospects of corrupt practices, but goes against the ethos of extending participatory democracy.

Although the regime of Compulsory Competitive Tendering (CCT), which has dismantled many good and bad local public service providers alike, has been displaced by the system of 'Best Value', the latter has introduced more central prescriptions on what and how local authorities should act than ever before. If local authorities want additional resources to carry out their work, they cannot exceed central government guidelines but can seek to secure LPSAs (Local Public Service Agreements) with Whitehall Departments to gain extra funding in return for meeting additional performance targets. At the same time, locally based Training and Enterprise Councils are being transformed into local franchise operators of the national Learning and Skills Council. A similar pattern can be detected with a nationally operated network of Small Business Services, a nationally run Youth Justice Board which decrees how local agencies must join up to form Youth Offending Teams, and a nationally directed network of Primary Care Trusts to take on the commissioning role for NHS services.

Towards a New Local-Central Relationship

To point to the proliferation of central initiatives is not to suggest that they do not have a role to play. Market deregulations have damaged social cohesion so severely that any responsible government would want to take swift restorative action. The problem is that a centralised state acting in isolation, without the informed participation of citizens in the public domain, leads inevitably to a dislocation between public policies and the democratic support needed to sustain their implementation. Paradoxically, the more a government tries to move forward without engaging the wider citizenry, the more likely the public will take things for granted and hold back from giving their share of contributions to support the government's agenda. Unless a government wants to hold power solely by feeding off the main populist sentiments which simply aggregate the unreflective views of individuals, it must engage citizens in thinking, discussing, and prioritising public policy options so that they can identify with policy selections which impact on their collective well-being.

One of the biggest difficulties in the UK is that it has historically subscribed to a false dichotomy regarding the local-central relationship. Successive governments have assumed that they must either surrender central controls to local institutions or strengthen the former at the expense of the latter. What is urgently needed is a strategic reorientation of this country's mode of governance so that whilst we render to the centre what is most effectively carried out by the institutions of central government, we allow local democratic bodies to attain true autonomy so that they can function as the civic focus of local communities in which citizenship has its roots.

Towards an Integrated Government Service (IGS)

People are most likely to become involved in civic deliberations through local democratic institutions, but they will continue to be reluctant to participate if they perceive all those institutions as mere puppets of decision-making processes centralised in Whitehall. This can be overcome if an honest appraisal is undertaken to identify what public services are so strategically critical that they must be run centrally for the whole country, and what public policy and service issues can be left to local bodies to determine in response to local needs. Up to now, the tendency is for the central government, on the one hand, to impose statutory duties and budgetary controls on local public bodies and yet to insist, on the other hand, that the local bodies should become champions of the interests of their local communities and develop their own policy agenda. For local bodies, be they the education, health, housing, or police authorities, the centre's call for greater community involvement rings hollow when it is repeatedly contradicted by directives which override local preferences.

A truly Integrated Government Service (IGS) would bring all public functions and services which require a strategic uniformity in command and control across the whole country under the central government. Citizenship would be enhanced because the accountability of government activities would become much sharper. For vital services such as child protection, for example, central government would no longer be able to hide its responsibilities for either inadequate policies or deficient funding by blaming what had hitherto been presented as 'independent' agencies. Equally, local social services committees which had in the past been torn by rising local demands for support and dwindling funding from the centre would move into a new era of transparent accountability. Elements which central government wants to take control of will be transferred openly, ending intervention by stealth as well as denial of responsibility by proxy. It cannot be denied that many public services have not realised their potential synergy because they operate without any well defined common agenda. What is important is to recognise that if there is to be direction from the centre on what that common agenda is to be, then the centre must make it clear that it is to be held to account for what it entails.

The establishment of IGS would not be incompatible with service responsiveness. It is sometimes argued that centralisation would mean that service delivery cannot be adapted to local circumstances. This confuses managerial autonomy with political accountability. Large multi-national corporations have shown how they can centralise control of the strategic and financial decisions of subsidiary operations and yet focus the latter on improved customer responsiveness. Yet precisely because being looked after as a customer does not imply having the slightest influence on the corporate governance of such remote corporations, an IGS can combine responsive service delivery and centralised political control. We will turn to what public services are to be in the local domain, but whatever is in the IGS would be the political responsibility of central government, and citizens would be able to judge its performance unequivocally.

The likely impact of IGS on public servants is something which can be easily overlooked. Public servants are citizens themselves, living not in some transcendental realm detached from the private sphere of everyday lives, but in communities which experience and react to the consequences of public policy decisions. For those who have been working in the twilight zone of quasi-centralised local public bodies, the clashes between the expectations of locally elected politicians and the instructions from central government have at times bred cynicism infecting friends, families and others with whom they come into contact. If they, working in organisations charged with delivering the services for the good of all citizens, feel that they are caught up in confusion, blurred accountabilities, and conflicting priorities, it is not surprising that others in their communities get the impression that 'public service' is not something which commands confidence, let alone their civic loyalty. Interestingly, in the UK, public opinion surveys have consistently shown that although there is almost always net satisfaction with the individual services provided by the overwhelming majority of local councils, in most local authority areas the public tends nonetheless to be dissatisfied with their councils. If they are satisfied with nearly everything these local bodies are responsible for, why are they unhappy with them overall? The answer lies in the paucity of public understanding of what they really do. They do not connect them with the services which they are satisfied with, but they readily blame them for problems which have nothing to do with them. Local public servants, disorientated themselves as to which set of political masters they are serving, offer little help to others in their respective communities. An IGS would go a long way towards bringing clarity to who should be blamed, and indeed praised, for what, and in time restoring pride in those who carry out public services, which in turn will help attract the interest and involvement of those who receive these services as citizens.

Undoubtedly one of the most forceful reasons to be put forward against the proposed approach would be that of costs. Any major restructuring of government services would have significant financial implications. But this obvious fact has not stopped numerous restructuring in the past—some successful and others utterly wasteful. The key question is whether it would lead to improvements which would more than outweigh the costs. Even on financial grounds alone, the establishment of an IGS would bring benefits which can be readily anticipated. At the most basic level, the twin funding of local government and police authorities through central revenue allocation and local taxation has created a complex industry of tracking and disputing funding support which generates unnecessary costs, exacerbates inefficiencies, and multiplies audit burden. The centre complains that the local bodies spend their allocations from Whitehall unwisely and warns them against raising too much from local taxation to make up the difference. The local bodies contest that the centre has failed to allocate sufficient money to carry out the statutory requirements the centre itself has imposed on them, while they protest that they are restrained from raising the revenue to meet the demands of local electorate. At the next level, with the increased recognition for better co-operation between branches of government separated by quasi-local autonomy, new directives are flying around to promote joined-up policies across health authorities, police authorities, probation services, education authorities, housing authorities, and many more. A corollary of this is a web of reapportionment of costs between partners who must guard against the diversion of their precious budgets beyond their respective remits.

In addition to the financial considerations, the benefits of integrating compartmentalised central government services, especially those hitherto hidden away in supposedly locally based bodies, are not difficult to see. Citizens' perception of the performance of the state is closely linked to their understanding of what is being delivered and who should be held accountable. At present, many of them still believe that it is futile to express their views because, for example, no one at their local council would listen to them when they complained about their local hospital. Since local councils do not have any constitutional, financial, or organisational basis to shape the way a local hospital is run, they should not be presented as somehow 'joined-up' to the latter. It would make more sense, managerially, politically and to the public, for vital social care elements to be integrated with the National Health Service as part of the IGS. Politicians always talk about cutting down red tape and reducing state bureaucracies. An exercise which brings out all those aspects in local public bodies which are controlled by statutory duties into an integrated structure which the centre has to account for directly would transform those scattered elements into a streamlined and transparent organisation for all citizens to access and evaluate.

Local Community-based Authorities (LCA)

If central government takes direct control of all those functions and duties which it has created a statutory responsibility to carry out, would there be anything left for local, community-based, public institutions to do? The answer is a resounding 'yes'. The latest Local Government Act has taken a major step in moving beyond the British constitutional paranoia which up to now has uniquely in the developed world restricted locally elected government to doing only what it has been given the power to do. In other Western democracies, local authorities can do whatever they are not explicitly forbidden by law to do. The Local Government Act grants local authorities in the UK a general power to promote the social, economic and environmental well-being of their local communities. The scope of this power can be largely determined by locally elected representatives in discussion with local citizens. This in effect means that local authorities can engage in an extensive range of activities to promote the collective well-being of their areas. Nor would this be a completely new experience in terms of being able to do what is not required by law to do. It should be remembered that even within the narrow constitutional framework of the UK, local authorities have over decades accumulated many discretionary powers granted by successive governments. This reflects the recognition by all political parties that there are benefits for all citizens if local authorities can exercise certain powers without central government insisting on how or when they are to be exercised. This is now being taken to its logical conclusion so that local authorities can do whatever it deems appropriate so long as it does not violate any specific law in so doing.

Only two factors stand in the way of practice fitting in with this logic. The first, concerning the burden imposed by centrally determined duties and targets, we have already addressed through our proposal to create an IGS. The second is about financial controls. Up to now, the tentacles of central government have reached inextricably into local public bodies, and the tax revenue, borrowing and expenditure plans of the latter have to be taken into account in national budget decisions. The result is detailed controls of what money local authorities can raise and spend, driven primarily by national, and not local, considerations. If, as it is proposed, whatever functions central government needs to have direct control over are transferred into an IGS, then there is no case left to retain the stringent financial controls. In short, we should see the liberation of local authorities to become fully fledged local community-based authorities (LCA). Given the ability to raise their own revenue to meet their respective local needs, LCAs would attract the interest of local citizens.

Contrary to a commonly held suspicion that political centralisation has already reached such a point that nothing would be left for local institutions to do, there are countless important matters for LCAs to deal with. Leaving the obvious life and death issues, basic subsistence which must be guaranteed for all, and fundamental rights of protection and security to the IGS, there would still be many quality of life factors which are of great concern to local communities. Examples would include: environmental enhancement of residential neighbourhoods and town/city centres; street lighting to promote a greater sense of community safety; local transport schemes to reduce the dependence on private vehicles; community events to bring people together; better opportunities to develop cultural, sporting, artistic and intellectual abilities; support for local heritage; advice to young people; and improved services for the elderly. None of these would be prescribed by the centre. Instead they would be determined by local citizens who will see their participation in democratic elections and consultation directly shape the policy and service outcomes.

The current system has for too long masked many pressing issues which local communities would keenly address if they had the freedom to do so. The control over education budgets—leading from time to time to the centre announcing a level of pay rise for teachers which cannot be funded from the inadequately financed budget—has meant that despite the widespread recognition that the number of detached youth workers (the professionals who have the skills and experience to go out to engage and support young people who would not otherwise seek advice from anyone) has already gone down too excessively, the youth service is the one which continues to see its resources depleted to fund the shortfall in other education activities. The same has happened with the community development work of social services which traditionally has played an important role in helping groups in the community build up social networks for mutual support. This service has suffered because with tax revenue capped by central government, the limited income (again determined by central government grant) has to be used to fund life and death priorities such as child protection. With IGS taking direct and transparent responsibility for those aspects of education and social services which central government has understandably wanted to have tight control over, LCAs would be able to respond to their respective communities in developing and delivering the youth support and community development services they want and are prepared to pay for through local taxation.

The close links between local tax payments to and the activities of LCAs would help local citizens develop their awareness and appreciation of what their LCAs do on their behalf. Instead of tax money always being paid into a remote state machine, the civic value of paying one's local taxes would be demonstrated by the LCA one can hold visibly to account in one's community. As for the number of layers of LCAs there should be, that would be a question for local people to determine rather than central prescription. In different areas, there would be different needs and views about whether there should be more strategic bodies above the district/borough level. Indeed, beyond that there would be the question of democratic regional assemblies. Local citizens should be allowed to decide if they want wider strategic issues—not dealt with under central government's jurisdiction—to be addressed by LCAs acting as a federation, by regional LCAs directly elected, or not at all. Such an approach would engage the interest of local people much more than simply as a proposition in a referendum called by central government.

The Balance between Minimum Standards and Democratic Diversity

The establishment of democratically autonomous LCAs would raise the question of whether our country can tolerate different levels of public service provision. The expression 'postcode lottery' has been coined deliberately to suggest an inherent arbitrariness in geographical service diversity. The intended impression is that people could end up receiving quite different public services simply because they live in different areas. This implies, however, that such democratical diversity is intolerable. The real question which needs to be answered is whether all public services are of a nature that they must be uniformly provided across the country or not at all, regardless of varying local needs and commitments. Of course there are services which should have minimum standards set and guaranteed for everyone across the country. This, as we have argued, is where the IGS has a vital role to play. But even the most ardent centralist could hardly sustain the insistence that beyond such services there could be no conceivably legitimate public service at all.

The public policy and service issues we have looked at in relation to LCAs illustrate that there are concerns which local people may have, and yet there need not be any standard solution to them across the country. It is the belief that no community of citizens can ever devise fair and effective solutions to the local problems they face which cuts at the roots of democracy and vibrant citizenship. In real communities, there are constantly issues which can be, and should be, dealt with without options being closed off for other communities. As citizens of the UK, we are all entitled to the same level of medical care if admitted in an emergency case. But if we had LCAs, some might decide in response to local demands to provide a supplementary service in their areas in the form of an assistant accompanying the discharged patient home to check if everything is in order for, not just a speedy, but comfortable recovery. If the citizens of a community believe they should pool their resources to ensure this can be achieved for everyone in their community, why should it not be allowed just because other communities may not want the same enhanced quality of life for themselves? It could be argued that at some point, national politicians may feel that it would be unfair on other communities and they would then want to introduce it for all parts of the country. That would be a matter for a national democratic debate. If the initiatives which different communities can develop through their own LCAs can prompt wider thinking and development of public policies across the country, that would be another reason for, not against, the spread of local diversity.

Accountability and Responsibility of Government and Public Bodies

ANTHONY BARKER

'Accountability' and 'responsibility' are key concepts in any attempts to achieve a more active and participative political culture. Democratic government rests upon them, albeit in their many versions and meanings: they are almost as flexible in their use and misuse as 'democracy' itself. Government is expected to have a positive and sensitive relationship with the private citizen, whether labelled as local resident, public service-user or customer. An active citizenship would seem certain to extract more political accountability and responsibility from both central and local government, including any amount of quangos.

At the macro level, the majority party in both the Commons and town halls are at real risk of being thrown out of office by their electorates for perceived serious failures in policy or conduct, as the Conservatives' national rout in 1997 and various local elections have confirmed to all parties. This traditional 'macro' of political representative democracy, based on the fear of election losses, must be considered alongside novel, 'micro' ideas for a more participative political culture, not least because one citizen's established right to exact general and ultimate responsibility from politicians through the ballot box might be prejudiced by another citizen's new and more particular and immediate claims on those leaders, using active methods of participation, possibly for sectional ends. Such prejudice or conflict between electoral and activist approaches to political responsibility may appear at any level or context within the wider political system. This chapter about central government should therefore be read with others in this book dealing with inter-party electoral politics; intra-party policy-making; parliamentary politics and procedural reforms; the new forms of Scottish and Welsh government; and elected local government. The 'strong government' tradition of British politics would ensure that any significant change in central government's core value or myth of responsibility to Parliament would promptly affect these other fields of government and politics.

Official Accountability: Insiders vs. Outsiders?

Politically active, participating citizens exist at all levels of politics, from parish or street level to a business tycoon who spends millions of his firm's money on political lobbyists and press officers to advance its commercial interests in the corridors of Whitehall and the mass media. If our theme is the politically demanding private interest—whether an individual citizen or an

© The Political Quarterly Publishing Co. Ltd. 2001
Published by Blackwell Publishers, 108 Cowley Road, Oxford OX4 1JF, UK and 350 Main Street, Malden, MA 02148, USA

association of them—then both 'top' and 'bottom' of a notably politically hierarchical and elitist governing system must be held in view. Broadly, the local activities and demands of residents, voluntary associations and traders are directed at elected local government itself and at appointed local bodies (local quangos) such as NHS trusts or further education colleges. In sharp contrast, the nationally active citizens aim at the central government and its national-level quangos. Even when they operate in local branches (of rival political parties or national interest groups, such as pro- and anti-hunting) they are consciously part of national opinion or campaigning designed to influence the current government or opposition to get a more favourable national policy. The important national activism is at firmly national (London) level, however. National associations of all kinds, from the most specialist interests to the CBI or TUC, try to lock into the relevant sections of Whitehall and Parliament in a standing relationship with them. The currency used is not the crude political threat of pressure (so that the term 'pressure group' is quite unsuitable) but useful technical information, legitimacy of interest, reasonable conduct, mutual respect and (as a result) a degree of trust which may allow hypothetical, exploratory negotiations on a 'without prejudice' basis. Acknowledged expertise, professional status, trustworthiness and a genuinely representative basis are four characteristics which not even the richest organised interest group can buy, although some of them may be achieved over time with regular investment and effort.

In considering how a more democratic system of government in Britain could be encouraged, some distinction should be made between making government more open as a system and more persuadable on particular policy merits. More inexperienced and lower status associations of active citizens may emphasise their need for more open government. As outsider groups they understand both the workings of government and the policy context of their particular needs and demands much less than the more experienced and more insider-style groups. As a result the outsider groups sometimes seem naively to assume that if only the world of government was more open to them (more transparent and less 'bureaucratic' in its processes) it would more readily meet their policy demands. In contrast, the group which is (or would like to become) an insider group naturally has little interest in openness, so long as it can get the internal information it needs to make its case to Whitehall. An effective insider group usually has resources (often technical information about its field or its corporate members) to offer Whitehall and it receives insider status in exchange. It is normally closely consulted on its direct views and interests and may, as we have noted, even be trusted. Such a group may well resent any greater openness in government because this reform would probably entail more standardised procedures, greater publicity and a more equal treatment of private organised interests. Those who already have their feet under one or more of Whitehall's many tables concentrate on gaining their policy goals and prefer to keep the details of their success as private as their privileged relationship with the key senior officials in their particular Whitehall patch. Knowing how Government and Parliament work, these inside groups do not attribute Whitehall's delay or opacity to a generalised 'bureaucracy' but appreciate the need for Whitehall's inter-departmental consultations, Treasury consent and the clearing of political lines between MPs, peers and party committees. Their task is to try to influence these internal processes by offering the information, briefing or arguments which each section and stage of government policy-making may require.

Accountability as 'Customer Relations'

The active citizen is both a potential consumer and a potential critic of the laws, administrative systems and public services which the executive and legislative sides of both central and local government jointly provide. Most of the concern with 'citizen participation', since that term arose in the 1960s, has been with people having more influence or even some control over public services which they personally consume or use. The term has not usually applied to more general democratic rights to criticise the central or local government on policy issues which do not particularly affect the critics themselves. To give examples, 'citizen participation' has typically referred to local residents concerned with improving their own housing, neighbourhood, traffic or school conditions. While policy criticism also covers these local issues, it more often runs to indivisible policy questions such as air pollution or the value for money being obtained by public expenditure.

In pursuing either consumerist or general critical objectives, the active citizen has somewhat different priorities which may entail some conflict of interests or goals. The plainest example is the proper treatment of casework decisions which arise from implementing any practical service delivery. What treatment are the properly self-interested, active citizens entitled to when seeking their share of a public service (such as a pension or benefit payment) or when receiving a compulsory official service such as official planning, safety or environmental consents when extending their home or business premises?

The most elementary entitlement is what any commercial firm would consider to be good customer relationships: a positive, responsive reaction to the public's enquiries, service requests and complaints. This is a question of the manner, not the substance, of response and, indeed, is best tested in cases where any claim to entitlement or request for favourable discretion is actually refused. While being disappointed or even made angry by a negative decision, has the citizen any fair criticism of the manner of their treatment?

The answer would probably turn on the next level of entitlement: the transparency of the decision. Making government and its satellite public bodies 'more transparent' has long been a buzz word of the private sector-style 'new public management' reform which has affected Britain more than any other country in Europe or North America. Its meaning is not quite the same as 'more open' because openness may imply a decision being actually made in the open. (It is this idea which leads some experienced decision-makers simply to dismiss open government as a contradiction in terms.) A transparent decision is, rather, one whose steps and processes are fully explained without the final stage being fully exposed to its formal recipient (the customer or user) or to any third party. Like good customer relations, transparent decision-taking by an official body is a matter of form and presentation.

Accountability and Reasoned Decisions

The substance of the active citizen's entitlement to the democratic character of an official decision is firmly engaged when the next stage of quality is claimed: the openly reasoned decision. There is, so far, no general legal duty on British central or local government, or on statutory or other public bodies, to give the reasons for their decisions. There has, of course, been the steady rise of judicial review of the quality of all important potential decisions by bodies exercising public functions (including private bodies such as universities and trade unions). It is well known that a high court judge may, subject to appeal, cancel an official decision which is not based on the relevant known rules or expectations for that type of decision; which seems illogical or incoherent in its own terms; or which is so clearly lacking in its honest application of some policy or decision-principle to the facts of the case that it is 'Wednesbury-unreasonable' (citing a classic early case) or, more plainly, perverse.

These judicial requirements for a judge-proof quality of decision have advanced steadily over roughly the last twenty-five years and may bound further ahead now that the European Convention on Human Rights (Council of Europe) has been incorporated into UK domestic law, under the Human Rights Act, and a new package of 'fundamental rights' promoted by the European Union. However, the further advance of UK judicial review of official decisions is likely to be gradual. The judges will probably continue to claim that they are not re-taking a decision on its merits but only checking on the decision's necessary characteristics. With a few exceptions, this claim will continue to be generally accepted as genuine and correct. A general legal duty on bodies exercising public functions to give reasons for decisions may be created by the courts as part of the rising demands of judicial review. Some experts in public law either support or simply expect this while senior civil servants, local government officers and quango officials may dread it.

The nature of this idea is plain in those public policy fields, such as land-use planning, where some degree of reason-giving has long been required. Any 'citizen' (whether an individual local resident or a major private firm) is entitled to seek planning permission on any land and to receive the local government's 'reasons for refusal' if consent is refused or limited by conditions. The applicant may appeal to central government and must provide 'grounds for appeal' on which the local decision-takers can comment to the government official (a planning inspector) who will decide or recommend an appeal decision to be taken by, or on behalf of, the central government. The inspector must compose either a decision letter or a much fuller report and recommendation to the central government (on planning appeals in England, this is the Department of the Environment). In the latter cases (or where the Department had called in the decision for its own determination) a similar decision letter will be issued by the Department following a minister's approval. On points of law, including any judicial review-type issues, an appeal then lies to the courts. The courts recognise that issuing planning consents and refusals and having them appealed to and largely decided by individual planning inspectors are both administrative, rather than judicialised, decision systems. Key documents such as planning consents and inspectors' decision letters are not analysed as if they were Acts of Parliament.

Coherent reason-giving by local planners and inspectors is required, however, and appeal decisions must be taken again if an inspector's decision letter is found to be significantly faulty. In such a subjective field as the planning and architectural design of buildings, this requirement of reason-giving can survive only if rather bare outline statements are allowed to pass as 'reasons'. Whatever the case may be for requiring reasons for all British public function decision-taking, it would be of no use to citizens as consumers or users to be told, in effect, that their application for some favourable discretion had failed because it did not meet the established standard. They will have realised that and want to know exactly why and how each part of their case failed each specified test. In one leading planning case the Law Lords (the UK's supreme court) had to judge the adequacy of a reason for a particular planning decision which had balanced the quality of new architectural design against that of protected historic buildings. They decided it was adequate if the decision letter clearly preferred one over the other on the particular 'facts' of that planning and architectural dispute and in the particular townscape context of that part of the City of London. To 'go behind' such a stated reason as this and to seek out what were called in this case 'the reasons for the reasons' would be unacceptable because it would make the land-use planning decision system impractical. In effect, a clear and coherently presented conclusion to a disputed case is taken to be the reason for the decision.

If government and bodies with public functions were required, as a new principle of public law, to give even rather outline or formulaic reasons for all their casework decisions, the sometimes flexible and discretionary nature of British public administration would need to move towards a more Continental, American judicialised style, based on published formal rules, criteria and processes. It would be a major blow to the British empirical, 'common sense' psychology of decision-taking, where merits rather than applied principles are uppermost and the paternalist power of the sensible and humane administrator to exercise favourable discretion is cherished as a

136

pillar of public service professionalism by the decision-takers themselves. The blow would probably be so great as to make any government try to legislate to cancel the judges' new-found powers.

Accountability and Appeals

A fourth level of an official decision's potential democratic quality is its being made subject to a right of formal review or appeal. As with legal appeals in the courts, this right may be restricted to appealing against alleged breaches of the rules or process involved, rather than the adverse decision on the case's merits. An internal review of a case (on either process or merits) by a more senior official is currently offered within, for example, social security benefits casework. Such a review is not formally independent of the authority which made the original adverse decision. In practice, however, a senior official is independent of a subordinate's earlier judgement and is quite free to reverse it, within current policy. Appeals to independent persons (for example an immigration arbitrator or appeal tribunal) against a government decision would appear a more robust and democratic device. But they may also be constrained by policy limitations and, indeed, should be so if casework decisions are not to become wildly inconsistent and the policy in question (for which the Department's ministers are responsible to Parliament and the public) not shot to bits. Individual citizen's rights to an independent appeal against an adverse official decision may conflict with general citizens' rights to know what policy or practice is in force, subject only to change through public argument and accountability.

The key terms for discussion of 'active citizenship' and political account-ability and responsibility need definition and some unpacking. Is 'active citizenship' merely better-informed and more confident, self-interested claim-making on public resources? Even if it does manage to be more 'responsible' than this, should it go beyond (advisory) 'citizen participation' into (execu-tive) 'citizen control' of any public services? If so, new local bodies such as budget-holding NHS community health councils or citizen juries, with actual decision powers (for example on local land planning casework or policy issues) would take over from the NHS officials and planning inspectors who currently act under their responsibility to Health and Environment ministers (who are in turn accountable and ultimately responsible to the House of Commons). Most of such transfers of actual powers would be from elected local government councillors and their officers rather than from ministers and their civil servants.

There is no logical connection between voters becoming better politically informed and more politically active. A person may be either well-informed or ignorant and also either active or inactive. Neither is 'active citizenship' necessarily on a higher moral or more 'responsible' plane than mere voting. An active and an inactive citizen may both be highly objective in their support for the wider public good, or the exact opposite.

Accountability and responsibility are different concepts, despite their increasing use as identical ones. For a politician or public official to be obligated by law or custom to 'give account' to a body or the public at large implies a requirement of openness, explanation, the honest answering of questions and criticisms and engagement in debate—plus, ideally, the often neglected follow-up process which allows critics to learn how some policy or promise turned out at a future regular meeting. These qualities have been labelled here 'good customer relations' and 'transparency'.

By contrast, 'responsibility' should be reserved for the politician's or official's formally determining relationships with their political superiors. On these occasions, their explanations could lead to an instruction to change the policy line or some particular decision on the understanding that any reluctance or disobedience would risk a transfer, suspension or even the requirement to resign or be dismissed.

Accountability is a broader, softer and more malleable concept than this line-of-command *determining responsibility*. It is therefore of much more use in an elaborate political system and culture where public policy issues seem to become ever more elaborate and conditional. It is helpful to consider both formal *upwards accountability* to a controlling authority (which is really the same thing as 'determining responsibility') and *downwards accountability* (which is often less formally based, offering open explanation and a chance to raise questions and criticisms, as just mentioned). A third useful term is *outwards accountability* whereby a public body or office-holder offers and receives *mutual accountability* to and from other relevant players in the public (and even the private) sector, to form a network of open, discursive relationships aimed at tackling public policy problems. Current attempts by central government to get local NHS and local authority social services (and also social services and police) to co-operate more effectively are examples of how a more formal regard for regular mutual accountability could assist better services. No formal orders can flow between these different public authorities but the ideas of mutual and explanatory accountability are most valuable. Another distinction lies between having strong *ex-ante accountability* (such as an elaborate planning inquiry into a proposed building or road project) and strong *ex-post accountability* and *responsibility* of official policy choices and casework decisions. *Ex-post* consideration is pretty weak in British government and a more active citizenship culture might help to protect us from serious accidents or obvious policy failures.

A radically more participative political culture would certainly affect the conduct of local government by elected councillors and their senior officers. But what of ministers and civil servants, given the symbolic weight of the so-called 'constitutional doctrine of the individual responsibility of ministers' to offer to resign when seriously wrong acts or omissions by their Departments are revealed? This 'doctrine' is better described as a 'working myth' in that it has no historical empirical substance; is forcefully rejected by ministers caught in this position; and is seen by informed observers of the various failures or scandals in question as irrational and actually damaging to the public interest. But, like any genuine myth, it still retains a meaning or function and certainly affects ministers' and officials' actual conduct of government—albeit often in a negative and even damaging way.

It is suggested that the tradition or myth of ministerial responsibility to a formally sovereign House of Commons—for all its mythical and politically manipulated character—would prove a much harder nut for some new style of 'active citizenship' to crack than would the operations of local government. This would not only be because more participative citizens would be more often interested in local government functions. Local NHS, social security, job training, further education and other fields run directly (or funded) by central government would be protected from greater direct citizen influence (and certainly from direct citizen power) by a powerful alliance. This would consist of ministers themselves and their civil servants (determined to maintain their national status and wider responsibilities); MPs (keen to conserve their now significantly dwindling political estate, as they see UK government powers being detached to the European Communities, Edinburgh, Cardiff and, perhaps before long, to at least some English regions); and all of the national organised interest groups (notably professional cadres such as doctors and lawyers) which gather round central government to offer technical information and advice in exchange for influence within Departments and national status within the wider political system.

Active Citizenship and Explanatory Accountability

The best hope for a new 'citizenship culture' to make an impact on central government is to ally itself to the lobby for serious parliamentary reform (such as it is) and join in pressing ministers and officials for richer *explanatory accountability* which does not challenge the constitutional positions of ministers, officials and MPs. As well as supporting the more elaborate and self-confident forms of parliamentary select committee work which both Houses of Parliament should develop, this new style of popular interest in policy issues should also help the steady development of the official public inquiry as the new political institution that it has become. To attempt this would be hard work because major public inquiries now reflect (and even themselves stimulate) a much more sophisticated and elaborate view of the issues (for example BSE or major fatal accidents such as the Sheffield football disaster or the King's Cross London tube fire) than anyone in government or politics has ever been used to.

Participatory citizen politics will not replace or even much affect the central government's relation to Parliament, the media or the voter. The mass politics of election manifesto mandates and the parties' traditional role of aggregating overlapping sectional interests and their salient issues offer a general democratic defence against the probably sectionalist and possibly self-serving 'active citizens' whose efforts may contribute to greater social, economic and environmental inequalities. Broadly speaking, electors (or 'citizens') would not trust each other to take actual decisions (as opposed to offering opinions) on public affairs—and particularly not where public money was to be allocated. Only elected representatives would be granted that authority because only they can be held responsible through the ballot box. Until they got themselves elected, even the most active of citizens would remain firmly on the 'citizen participation' side of the fence, urging their views and priorities on to their elected representatives or the relevant officials. No elected councillor or MP will vote to give decision powers to unelected persons, nor to allow a government-appointed public body (quango) to cut itself free from ultimate government control while it exercises public powers, using public money. Ministers' responsibility to MPs to keep control of the government and its offshoots serves as a guide to MPs at the next election, particularly, of course, if the Member has been sitting on the government benches.

There is quite a lot which more active citizens could do to help improve the quality of the linkage between ministers, their party, MPs on all sides, the serious media (such as they nowadays are) and the voter or citizen. There is also, as already suggested, much that MPs could and should insist on doing to improve their performance in extracting more and better quality for an explanatory accountability (and perhaps some further elements of a deter- mining responsibility) from ministers, their senior officials and their quango appointees. Of course, a more educated, interested, active and public interest- minded electorate would stimulate many improvements in both central and local government, so long as the system's basic democratic theory is not weakened. The fundamental process of holding governments to their deter- mining responsibility to the electorate will not and should not be much altered by a change to a new, popular grass-roots political culture or style— however attractive it may seem to be on its own terms. There is no substitute for the familiar 'promise-performance' reckoning between a government and the electorate which faces all administrations at least every five years.

Citizenship in Britain: Attitudes and Behaviour

PATRICK SEYD, PAUL WHITELEY and CHARLES PATTIE

'I know from my postbag how much disillusionment about the political process there is among the general public. The level of cynicism about Parliament, and the accompanying alienation of many of the young from the democratic process, is troubling. It is an issue on which every member of the House should wish to reflect. It is our responsibility, each and every one of us, to do what we can to develop and build public trust and confidence.' (House of Commons Official Report, 26 July 2000, Cols 1113–4)

SENTIMENTS such as those quoted above, contained in Betty Boothroyd's retirement speech as Speaker of the House of Commons, are now common and reflect an elite-level concern that all is not well with the body politic. Various measures of mass-level attitudes and behaviour suggest that this concern is well founded. First, the public today has less confidence in, trust of, and respect for political institutions and politicians than previous generations. Secondly, levels of political participation are declining. Electoral turnout at the 1997 general election was lower than for any of the previous fourteen post-1945 elections. Low turnouts have also been the norm in recent elections of members of the European Parliament, local councillors, members of the sub-national Scottish, Welsh and London parliaments and assemblies, and the London mayor. Party membership has been dropping. Even Tony Blair's success in recruiting an additional 40 per cent of new members to the Labour Party between 1994 and 1997 has not been sustained. Also the numbers willing to serve on public bodies seems to be declining; for example, nowadays there are often difficulties in attracting people onto school governing boards or community health bodies. Thirdly, levels of political attachment are declining. One such example is the weakening of people's attachments to political parties. Data from the British Election Studies reveal that 44 per cent of voters described themselves as 'very strong' party identifiers in 1964, but by 1997 only 16 per cent declared themselves in such terms. It is claimed that 'over the three decades the electorate has moved from committed partisanship to semi-detached preferences'.[1]

There is no shortage of explanations for the public's decline in political trust, participation and attachment. One suggestion is that parties are no longer committed to definite and distinct principles. 'Parties and politicians are all the same' is a common refrain as Conservative and Labour parties scramble to occupy a common, consensual ground occupied by 'middle Englanders', 'Essex man' or 'Worcester woman' as revealed by focus groups and opinion polls. Furthermore, as the costs of fighting elections

© The Political Quarterly Publishing Co. Ltd. 2001
Published by Blackwell Publishers, 108 Cowley Road, Oxford OX4 1JF, UK and 350 Main Street, Malden, MA 02148, USA

escalate, parties and politicians need to solicit large sums of money from sources that may expect political favours in return. Today's politicians therefore appear to be more corrupt than their predecessors.

Another suggestion is the increasing powerlessness of governments. Globalisation arguably means that they have ceded their powers to multinational bodies, such as the European Union, the International Monetary Fund or the World Trade Organisation, and to multinational companies. A third suggestion is the breakdown of traditional community bonds. Individuals now lead more atomised and anonymous lives in which they are more likely to be watching television and 'bowling alone'[2] than participating in collective activities. A final suggestion is that a new, well-educated, and non-deferential generation has emerged whose levels of trust, participation and political attachments are significantly lower than previous generations.

This increasing elite-level concern with the decline in the public's levels of political trust and participation has prompted a range of initiatives from government and other bodies to remedy the situation. The government's White Paper on modernising local government[3] suggests various measures to encourage people to vote in local government elections, including electronic voting, mobile polling stations, voting extended over a number of days and entire elections conducted by postal ballots. In addition, the government has eased the restrictions on the use of postal votes in general elections in an attempt to raise voter turnout. Other initiatives to try and stimulate a greater interest in politics, and participation in particular, have come from the Citizenship Foundation, Common Purpose and the Institute for Public Policy Research.

The Economic and Social Research Council has initiated a 'Democracy and Participation' research programme to address 'a number of key concerns about the current state of British democracy and participation'. Twenty one research projects have been funded which address the question of political participation; in particular, they ask what participation is taking place? Why do some participate while others do not? What effects will the government's new constitutional reforms have upon participation? What are the links between participation, governance and democratic accountability? And, finally, is there a crisis of participation and democratic legitimacy in Britain?

One of the funded projects in this ESRC programme is a Citizen Audit which will collect data on the scope and determinants of citizen participation and attitudes to democracy in Britain. The aim of the audit is to address the question: 'what does it mean to be a citizen in modern Britain?' The answer to this question means probing theories of participation, examining citizen voluntary activities and public attitudes to government, politics and policy-making. While there is a rich literature addressing the theories of citizenship,[4] there have been few empirical studies of who participates in politics, why they participate, what are their forms of participation and how does this participation link to the state of British democracy. The last, and only extensive, national study of such participation was conducted in 1984 and the results were published eight years later.[5]

The Citizen Audit

The Citizen Audit is a stratified, random sample of 24,000 people in one hundred local authorities in England, Wales and Scotland, with 3,000 face-to-face interviews and 21,000 mail questionnaires. The reason for such a large sample size is to be able to measure and compare people's behaviour and attitudes in specific localities. It will be possible to ascertain the extent to which a person's place of habitation affects both behaviour and attitudes. Does citizenship differ among the English, Welsh and Scots? Does citizenship vary between those living in towns and cities and those living in rural areas? In addition, by also applying a range of measures of local service-delivery efficiency we can ascertain whether people's levels of citizenship are affected by the quality of their local services.

The face-to-face element of the audit is a panel survey so that, as well as taking an immediate health check on the state of British democracy, comparisons can be made of people's attitudes and behaviour over time. The first wave of the panel survey was completed at the end of the year 2000[6] and the second wave will go into the field after the general election. The panel design offers an opportunity to ascertain whether the general election has a significant impact upon citizenship and participation.

Participation takes many forms and in the audit we define it broadly in order to capture both orthodox and unorthodox, formal and informal, group and individual behaviour. However, we exclude participation for which the individual receives financial rewards, believing that it is unpaid participation that underpins democracy. So participation in the labour force is not included. The following are the forms of participation which the audit is attempting to measure. First, those belonging to, participating in, or donating money to a wide range of organisations. The questionnaire lists 26 distinct types of organisation, ranging across those representing specific demographic, social, cultural, recreational, occupational, religious and programmatic groupings. In addition, the audit includes those who participate in informal neighbourhood networks providing such services as meals-on-wheels, home visits, and personal shopping.

Secondly, the audit includes people who contact other people or organisations in order to influence political outcomes. For the majority of people their concerns revolve around everyday matters to do with their work, travel to work, health, living accommodation and, where appropriate, their children's education. We ask them about their experiences of the services closely related to these concerns and to what extent, if they have been dissatisfied, they have tried to influence service delivery. How did they do this? To whom did they make overtures?

Thirdly, the audit calculates the number of people identifying with issues and causes through a variety of actions such as voting in transnational, national or sub-national elections, marching, demonstrating or lobbying, purchasing or boycotting particular goods and services, wearing badges or placing posters, and donating or raising money. Finally, the audit measures a fourth form of participation, namely those serving the community in some form, such as being a school governor or a member of a community health council.

As well as measuring people's participation, the audit examines their sense of personal efficacy. To what extent do they believe that participation is worthwhile? Do they feel that the service professionals they come into regular contact with in, for example, schools, doctors' surgeries and hospitals, listen to and respond to their concerns? Do they feel they have the ability to participate in workplace decisions? Do they think that governments take note of their views? Do they believe the institutions of the state such as Parliament are working well or badly? Finally, the audit measures their tolerance of other people's opinions and behaviour, and their sense of obligation both to the state—by, for example, paying their taxes and by obeying the law—and to other individuals—by, for example, helping their neighbours, by picking up litter, and by reporting crime.

Theories of Participation

The audit is designed in such a manner as to make it possible to examine rival theories of participation and to assess which of them provide the most plausible explanation of participation and non-participation. Here we highlight just three of these theories and examine some initial findings from the audit which throw light on the most well-known of these theories of participation.

Perhaps the most popular explanation of participation is the civic voluntarism model.[7] This theory explains participation in terms of three classes of factors: resources, motivations and mobilisation. With regard to resources such as money, education and time, the argument is that individuals with high socio-economic status and time on their hands are likely to participate more than low status, time-poor individuals. Motivation principally means the individual's sense of personal efficacy, or the extent to which they feel that they can make a difference to society by participating. Finally, mobilisation refers to the extent to which individuals are recruited into participating by other people, particularly family and friends. Studies of participation in Britain and the USA have claimed that high resources, strong motivation and mobilisation by others will produce participation.

One problem with this theory, however, is that the general expansion in educational standards should lead to higher rather than lower levels of participation and yet, as we mentioned earlier, political participation is declining. There is also the problem that many people with high socio-economic status do not participate in politics, preferring sports, cultural activities or home improvements. So the theory does not really explain why resources translate into political participation. Notwithstanding these points it is the most widely used theoretical explanation of political participation in the empirical literature.

There are alternative theories of participation based on social psychological variables or rational actor explanations. An example of the former is relative deprivation theory.[8] This explains protest behaviour in terms of the gap between individual expectations of income, status and benefits and what is actually received. The argument is that protest behaviour, involving activities like attending demonstrations, boycotting goods and civil disobedience, will be triggered by a significant gap between individuals' expectations and their experiences.

Rational choice explanations of participation suggest that individuals get involved if the benefits outweigh the costs. Benefits include private returns associated with enjoying participation for its own sake, developing friendships and other links with like-minded individuals. But they also include 'collective' benefits involving changing government policies or influencing public opinion over an issue.

Our own work has focused on explaining participation in political parties and is grounded in a general incentives theory. This is a hybrid theory combining social psychological factors and calculations of costs and benefits to explain why some people join political parties and become active once they have joined.[9]

Another important explanation of participation is grounded in sociological theories of citizen involvement and is based on the idea of social capital. Social capital refers to networks of civic engagement in society and levels of interpersonal trust which facilitate co-operation between individuals to solve collective action problems.[10] Recent work by Putnam in the United States suggests that social capital is very important for sustaining American society, but that it has been declining for some years.[11] The audit enables us to investigate this issue in Britain.

The Audit Findings

One major purpose of the audit is to provide basic information on people's participation in general. As mentioned earlier, one such measure of their participation is the extent to which they are involved with organisations. So we asked respondents to tell us whether they had paid a membership fee to an organisation, had participated in an activity arranged by an organisation, or had done voluntary or unpaid work for an organisation in the previous twelve months. These measures take us beyond the more passive form of participation which is to donate money to an organisation.

The audit reveals that a majority of people (57 per cent) are involved with organisations. Motoring organisations attract the single, largest number of participants (28 per cent), and almost all of them are members with very few taking part in, or providing voluntary work for these organisations. Clearly participation here is an instrumental action, a rational calculation of the benefits of membership. Similarly, large numbers (22 per cent) participate in gymnasia, sports and leisure organisations, and most, again, are members. Residential, housing and neighbourhood organisations attract the third largest group of people (13 per cent), but in these the levels of those taking part in, or providing voluntary work for, the organisations are higher than the levels of membership. Rather than taking out a membership subscription, people become involved in organisational activities. Finally, trade unions, churches, social clubs, and cultural groups attract the next largest numbers of participants (ranging from 9 to 7 per cent).

If we contrast the forms of organisational participation above (membership, participation and voluntary work) with donating money, the differences are striking. None of the organisations referred to above attract much in the way of financial donations. Instead, it is medical (36 per cent of respondents had donated), disabled (32 per cent), animal rights (24 per cent), ex-service (23 per cent) and pensioners (19 per cent) organisations which attract most people's donations.

Space considerations prevent us from exploring many of the explanations of participation referred to earlier in this article, but it is interesting to pursue the most common of the theories, namely civic voluntarism. To reiterate the earlier point, this theory explains political participation in terms of three factors. As Verba, Schlozman and Brady explain:

'We focus on three factors to account for political activity. We suggested earlier that one helpful way to understand the three factors is to invert the usual question and ask instead why people do not become political activists. Three answers come to mind: because they can't; because they don't want to; or because nobody asked. In other words people may be inactive because they lack resources, because they lack psychological engagement with politics, or because they are outside of the recruitment networks that bring people into politics.' (p. 269, op. cit.)

We asked our respondents whether, in the previous twelve months, they had attempted 'to influence rules, laws or policies' by utilising a range of options, including contacting politicians, organisations, public officials, the media, or legal personnel, signing a petition, taking part in a strike or a demonstration, and boycotting or buying certain products. Almost three quarters of our respondents (73 per cent) had engaged in some political influencing activity. As can be seen below, the most common of this type of political activity was signing a petition, followed by boycotting or purchasing particular products. Almost one in two had signed a petition, and one in three had boycotted a product. One in four had raised funds for an organisation or contacted a public official. One in eight had contacted a politician.

Question: *'During the last 12 months have you done any of the following to influence rules, laws or policies?'*

	% saying 'yes'
Signed a petition	41
Boycotted certain products	30
Raised funds for an organisation	28
Bought certain goods/products for political/ethical reasons	27
Contacted a public official	25
Worn/displayed campaign badge/sticker	21
Contacted a solicitor or judicial body	19
Contacted a politician	13
Contacted an organisation	11
Contacted the media	9
Attended a political rally/meeting	5
Taken part in a public demonstration	4
Taken part in a strike	2
Participated in an illegal protest	1

Is there any evidence that these political participants have a high socio-economic status, a strong sense of personal efficacy, and have been directly approached to become involved? If one simply distinguishes our professional and manual respondents, 85 per cent of the former, and 66 per cent of the latter, had been involved. Individuals with a higher socio-economic status appear to have more of the resources necessary to engage in political activity. Secondly, we measured our respondents' sense of political efficacy by asking them to respond on a five-point scale (strongly agree, agree, neither agree nor disagree, disagree, strongly disagree) to the statement that 'people like me can have a real influence on politics if they are prepared to get involved'. Among those strongly agreeing, 77 per cent had been involved in at least one of these political activities whereas only 62 per cent of those strongly disagreeing had been involved. Finally, we asked our respondents whether they had received a direct personal request to become involved in any of these political activities. Among those who had received such a direct personal request, 92 per cent took part, while of those who did not receive such a request, 66 per cent took part.

It would appear that the civic resources theory helps explain why some people are more politically active than others but what it does not explain is why those with fewer resources, a lower sense of motivation, and fewer mobilisation networks still participate. This provides a challenge which we can only resolve by testing some of the other theories of participation mentioned earlier.

Conclusion

Our initial, preliminary findings from the audit are that people's organisational commitments are extensive and range beyond donating money to

PATRICK SEYD, PAUL WHITELEY AND CHARLES PATTIE

donating time, effort and commitment. Taking into consideration people's activities in organised clubs, associations and groups and also in informal networks and neighbourhood support groups, one in three devote more than one hour each week of their time in this manner. Furthermore, when people were asked whether they would be willing to participate in various ways, those responding positively to serving on a jury (73 per cent), participating in a neighbourhood watch scheme (70 per cent), giving blood (68 per cent), helping renovate a local amenity (55 per cent), or assisting with meals on wheels (44 per cent) suggests a strong voluntary spirit among people. In addition, we have already noted the wide repertoire of political activities, particularly of the personal and informal type, in which people are engaged. Finally, the audit reveals that people's levels of personal trust in others are high; six in every ten people are trusting, and only one in ten are distrustful. Overall, therefore, the audit reveals relatively strong levels of social and personal capital. However, what does emerge from the audit is that one in three of our respondents are dissatisfied with democracy. Betty Boothroyd, and others like her, are right to be concerned about the levels of public disillusionment in the formal body politic.

Notes

1 I. Crewe and K. Thomson, 'Party Loyalties: Dealignmentor Realignment' in G. Evans and P. Norris, eds., *Critical Elections*, London, Sage, 1999.
2 R. Putnam, *Bowling Alone*, New York, Simon & Schuster 2000.
3 Department of the Environment, Transport and the Regions, 'Modern Local Government: In Touch with the People', 1998.
4 H. Van Gunsteren, *A Theory of Citizenship*, Boulder, Colorado, Westview Press, 1998.
5 G. Parry, G. Moyser and N. Day, *Political Participation and Democracy in Britain*, Cambridge, CUP, 1992.
6 The data which we report in this article are based upon the first wave of the face-to-face panel survey interviews. 3,140 interviews were conducted; we would stress the preliminary nature of our data at this stage.
7 G. Parry, G. Moyser and N. Day, op. cit.; S. Verba, K. Schlozman and H. Brady, *Voice and Equality: Civic Voluntarism in American Politics*, Cambridge, Mass., Harvard University Press, 1995.
8 W. G. Runciman, *Relative Deprivation and Social Justice*, London, Routledge, 1966; A. Marsh, *Protest and Political Consciousness*, London, Sage, 1977; T. Gurr, *Why Men Rebel*, Princeton, Princeton University Press,1970.
9 P. Seyd and P. Whiteley, *Labour's Grass Roots: The Politics of Party Membership*, Oxford, Clarendon Press, 1992; P. Whiteley, P. Seyd and J. Richardson, *True Blues: The Politics of Conservative Party Membership*, Oxford, Clarendon Press, 1994.
10 R. Putnam, *Making Democracy Work*, Princeton, New Jersey, Princeton University Press, 1993.
11 R. Putnam, *Bowling Alone*, op. cit.

The Divine Comedy of Contemporary Citizenship

COLIN CROUCH

For a mediæval Christian like Dante Alighieri the Church represented God's presence on earth, and the Pope was Christ's vicar. And yet it was possible for him to locate an individual pope, Boniface VIII, in the eighth circle of hell, excluded forever from divine grace on account of his sins of corruption. With such paradoxes must the mediæval man of principle wrestle; unable to renounce the institution and office which were God's representatives, but equally unable to abstain from moral judgement if those who held that office strayed from its sublime obligations.

Dante would have sympathised with the earnest citizen of the turn of the 20th and 21st centuries: totally committed to the values of the polis and the need to participate in civic duties, yet so often disillusioned at the petty or even squalid conduct of those elected or appointed to act as the embodiments of that polis. As many studies show us, including the chapters by Karen Evans and by Patrick Seyd, Paul Whiteley and Charles Pattie in this volume, increasingly people (especially younger ones) are resolving this dilemma by simply abandoning faith in the polis. Disillusioned with politicians, they denigrate the activity of politics itself, and shrink from participation in it. Of course, complaint about the cynicism of the political class can be self-serving. Disillusion can be merely a dignified form of idleness. Or people may simply be too busy earning a living and keeping their families together to have much time or thought left for public activity.

But, as Seyd, Whiteley and Pattie, and also Isobel Lindsay, show, many disillusioned citizens share the modern version of Dante's dilemma. They want to be fully committed to the values of the polis and to their personal responsibilities as a citizen. But they see elections slavishly imitating sales campaigns for goods and services, parties as little more than vehicles for the projections of their leaders' personalities, political communication as attempts at controlling and limiting the arena of free debate and sanitising all real conflict. They see the political class disappearing into a revolving-door network of advisers and corporate lobbyists which privileges the priorities of the latter, until both the policy formation and the funding of political parties follow the arts, sport, universities and almost everything else in becoming the grovelling clients of large corporations.

'If you feel like that you should try to change things!' is the conventional answer of the political establishment to such complaints. 'Unlike Dante you live in a democracy. Use the opportunities for participation which are open to you in our transparent information society!'

Published by Blackwell Publishers, 108 Cowley Road, Oxford OX4 1JF, UK and 350 Main Street, Malden, MA 02148, USA   149

'Participate how?' answers disillusioned youth: 'By voting in elections for a choice between parties which increasingly differ more in their presentation than their substance? By joining a party which will be seen by its leaders as either a flock of sycophantic cheerleaders or an irritating nuisance, to be rendered dispensable as soon as the flow of corporate campaign funding allows? By sending messages to party web sites managed by lower-level employees of spin doctors? Or by becoming a corporate lobbyist, waiting for the revolving door to come round, and hoping to hang on to my principles as I hurtle through it?' The official institutions of contemporary politics can resemble the mediæval Church in their inaccessibility as well as in their inability to be worthy of the task they bear.

Can we at least follow Dante in protecting our appreciation of the importance of politics and our obligations as citizens from our perceptions of the way in which political activity is conducted? This is not easy in a world where the personalisation of politics has increasingly become both the substitute for the differentiation of parties by policy difference and a means whereby politics can try to imitate some of the features that seem to make the world of entertainment so popular. It is, however, in trying to re-establish that distinction that our best hopes for saving the concept of active citizenship lie.

An important cause of the current malaise is that politics and discussion of it in the mass media are becoming increasingly self-referential: politics is about itself. Not surprisingly, large numbers of people feel that it has little to do with them. Politicians themselves are acutely aware of this, and blame the media for being obsessed with personalities instead of the great issues of the day. However, when it is so frequently obvious that politicians' own concern with the great issues is in using them to advance their own personalities and careers, it would be difficult for the media to do much about it, even if it wanted to.

There is nothing at all new in politics being self-referential; for centuries the world of courtly politics was precisely this. In the history of mediæval and early modern Europe politics as *citizenship* was to be found, as the origins of the word itself imply, in what we would today call local government: in the government of cities and communities, not in the courts of kings from which modern parliamentary government derives. It was the great processes of modernisation and the challenge of democratisation, from the late 18th to the mid-20th century, which really made national politics the serious public business which it seeks to be, and made both demands for and claims on citizenship. We need desperately to hold on to this as the great issues of modernisation quieten down and democracy becomes ambiguously both entrenched and tamed, ushering in a new era of place-seeking, courtly, politics at precisely the moment when the educational level of the mass electorate and its access to politically relevant information might promise a golden age of citizenship.

Two Models of Citizenship Promotion

To deal with these ambiguities we need to grade proposals for the strengthening of citizenship in two classes: those which are designed to strengthen the engagement of citizens in the established institutions of the polity; and those which seek to enhance citizens' capacities to act, without necessarily leading them to recognised channels. A mature citizenship requires both. The former by itself runs the risk of trying merely to cajole the population into taking more interest in the trivialised media spectacle currently offered to them—teaching them to accept Pope Boniface. The latter by itself threatens to create activists rather than citizens—heretics. I shall therefore here examine both, and their relationship to each other.

Promoting commitment to political institutions

'Don't vote! It only encourages them' ran an old anarchist graffito. The insight behind it is that politicians in democracies desperately need the electorate to take notice of them and sanction their existence. Voters in Florida might well warn the anarchist that this might be a complacent assumption: politicians might sometimes be in a position so to fix things that they would be happier if fewer citizens voted or had their votes counted. However, in general the anarchist's assumption is right; politicians worry dreadfully if the public becomes indifferent to them. (Look how angry they became when the commercial pressures, to which they had themselves exposed the broadcasting media, led to the television news broadcasts which they use to project themselves to us being shifted to unpopular viewing times.) This is not merely because their vanity requires that we pay attention to them: if discontent and emerging interests are not focused on the formal political world, which they understand and control, the threat of disorder looms. The world of established politics itself can therefore be expected to produce many useful ideas for promoting increased involvement in itself by citizens.

Several such are to be found in this volume, and together they provide a worthwhile and practical agenda for any reforming government. Martin Linton looks hard at the disincentives to vote embodied in the British parliamentary voting system. Matthew Taylor looks creatively at ways in which political parties at local level might rebuild their links with voters and communities. John Maxton updates the perennial agenda for House of Commons reform. Michael Brunson examines ways in which the mass media could play a more informative role. Henry Tam provides a refreshing new agenda for locally based government. Anthony Barker explores the scope for extending the concept of accountability in ways which would be useful to active citizens.

But none of these will do much to strengthen real citizen effectiveness if the political world to which they relate remains self-referential, manipulative and controlling in its relations to ordinary citizens, and seriously responsive only to business elites. However, it is likely that it will and even must remain like this. There are two kinds of party: those which are run by manipulative control freaks, and those which lose elections. There are two kinds of party conference: those which are sycophants of their leaders, and those which are dogfights between varieties of unrepresentative groups. There are two kinds of election campaigns: those lavishly funded by business, and those run on a shoe string. Trying to change these facts is a quixotic project. Rather, we must create alternative facts of which the strange hyper-professionalised world of contemporary politics is forced to take note: actions, demands, pressures to which it needs to respond for the sake of its own survival, but which it cannot incorporate and control, because they remain *autonomous and beyond its grasp*. Citizens must create a world of citizenship adjacent to, interacting with but remaining separate from formal political institutions themselves. This brings me to the second type of solution for strengthening citizenship.

Proposals for building active, autonomous citizens

Several of the contributors to this book make proposals for strengthening the capacities of the citizenry itself rather than its attachments to formal political institutions. This is seen first and foremost in Richard Pring's refreshing and wonderfully unfashionable celebration of the broad-based conception of education embedded in the work of the long since assassinated Schools Council. Tom Schuller's chapter on lifelong learning forms an appropriate complement. If, as an electorate, we could achieve the depths of political understanding such education programmes imply, we would be both less easily manipulated and more capable of formulating demands to the political system to which it had to make intelligent responses. Much the same is true for Anthony Everitt's discussion of culture as a source of opportunities for discovering autonomy, Isobel Lindsay's account of the voluntary sector, and Yasmin Alibhai-Brown's challenge on how we might move beyond multi-culturalism.

At first glance, Joyce McMillan's discussion of Scottish devolution belongs more in the first class of proposals, for strengthening the attachment of citizens to formal institutions. But what she in fact describes and celebrates is the challenge to the professionals by autonomous, creative social forces forging new collective identities.

Not only do we need ideas of these kinds for strengthening citizens as the active subjects rather than the passive observers of political action, but we must also reconsider its appropriate objects. Throughout the 20th century socialists sought how to achieve economic as well as political citizenship, from the concerns of the Webbs and of G.D.H. Cole with industrial citizenship to that of Will Hutton with the stakeholder economy. There is little of this in the agenda of the early 21st century, though it is now more urgent than ever before.

When capitalism approximates reasonably closely to the ideal of the free-market economy, with masses of producers in every market, all of whom are price-takers following the signals of consumer demand, there is strength in the economists' claim that there is no such thing as power in the market, and therefore no politics and no need for citizenship within its realm. But this can hardly be sustained for the contemporary phase of capitalism, dominated by global corporations. Many of these are certainly subject to competition in the strict economic sense, but they are not the passive price-takers of economic theory which they need to be to justify the claim that capitalist firms cannot present problems of political power.

The lobbying capacities of large corporations dominate the conduct of contemporary governments. Their capacity to choose the kinds of political regime in which they locate their activities, even if exaggerated by both themselves and their opponents, constitutes an extremely important form of political pressure. And the growing dependence on them of most non-commercial walks of life for sponsorship gives them a policy-making reach far beyond their core businesses and reaching to the heart of culture.

How the claims of citizenship can be reconciled with or incorporated into societies in which corporations frequently exercise more power of a political kind than governments is a fundamental question which is simply not being faced. If anything, as the concept of the sovereignty of shareholder value in the responsibilities of firms becomes a universal orthodoxy, we move further away from being willing to challenge it than at any time in the past century. In this collection of essays, only Karen Evans and Neal Ascherson face up to this directly, and then through only one—though a fundamentally important—aspect, that of work. It could be argued that to worry about improving the quality of formal political channels while doing nothing to constitutionalise lobbying and sponsorship processes is to strain at the gnat while swallowing the camel.

Moving towards a 'citizen culture', the concept on which this book is focused, requires, in addition to the reform of political institutions them-selves, consideration of both the educational and cultural state of citizens themselves, and an extended view of the institutions within which citizenship should be exercised.

Conclusions

But none of this means ignoring mainstream politics. Some participants in the Third Way debates of the late 1990s seemed to suggest that democracy might be better served by sophisticated opinion-polling, focus groups and govern-ment openness to widespread lobbying than by the conventional accoutre-ments of mass parties, elections and parliaments. This was a highly elitist view. Government and its advisers control the agenda of opinion polls and focus groups, and lobbying will always be dominated by business interests ahead of all others. Contemporary disillusion with party and electoral politics risks walking right into this elitist trap. This can be seen particularly in some strands of the social capital movement of contemporary American liberals, such as Robert Putnam, whose thinking has been useful to several of the present contributors. There is a danger of interpreting social capital in such a way that it advocates citizens turning aside from concern with the state and just doing things for themselves—a kind of collectivist neo-liberalism. But in the world of political do it yourself no voluntary or community activity will ever rival the scope of the giant corporations or dissolve the great body of power wielded by the state. Capitalists' complaints about government intervention in business do not mean that they do not want to intervene in government.

Today's citizens therefore need a very balanced position: addressing and engaging with the institutions of formal democracy, but retaining their autonomy from them and resisting their charmed embrace. The institutions do remain fundamental, which is why proposals for improving them are always welcome. But citizens should not believe that their duties are fulfilled by participating in parties, elections or other officially provided channels, as these have become highly controlled and limited. It is therefore in cause organisations which seek to change the political agenda that concerned citizens will increasingly be found. For those on the left this means such bodies as Charter 88, Friends of the Earth, campaigns for the Third World, and increasingly, as they are excluded from the political inner circle, trade unions. For those on the right it is presumably such groups as the Countryside Alliance.

In some ways, therefore, we remain in a similar position to Dante. There is no more possibility for the contemporary citizen to escape from the need to address the institutions of formal politics than there was for the mediæval Christian of evading the Church: *Salus extra ecclesia non est*. But when these essential institutions fail to be worthy of their role, our position is better than his; we do have the capacity to challenge. In his desperation to have the Church reformed, Dante, Guelph though his sympathies were, supported the Emperor in his wars against the Pope as a potential cleansing force for the Church, and was bitterly disillusioned by the outcome. Modern democratic citizens should not look to exogenous forces to resolve our discontents. We must take actions ourselves to forge and activate the external organisations which will try to press the polity. The richer the various forms of education for citizenship that exist, the stronger an autonomous culture capable of criticising both politics and business, more of us will be able to accept this challenge, rather than lapsing into either apathy or *incivisme*.

Index

accountability 7, 132–40
Adams, Rolan 50
Adenauer, Konrad 60
Advisory Group to the Secretary of State for Education and Employment 95–7
Alternative Vote 13–15
   see also Jenkins Commission
All Our Futures: Creativity, Culture and Education 71
Americanisation 4
appeals 137–9
Aristotle 65
arts 64–73
   and identity 65–6
   funding 68
   traditional participation 64, 67
Arts Council of Great Britain 54, 64, 65, 67, 73
Asian Dub Foundation 70
Australia 14, 16
Austria 79

BBC (British Broadcasting Corporation) 76, 77, 78–9, 80
   Radio 4 49, 54
Bell, Martin 22
Benelux countries 59
Blair, Tony 12, 13, 19, 49, 52, 77, 80, 141
Boniface VIII, Pope 149
Boothroyd, Betty 141, 148
Bosnia 74
Braden, Su 66
Brecht, Bertolt 65
British Council 54
British Election Studies 141
British identity 47–55
British Social Attitudes survey 92
Broadcasting Act (1990) 80
Broadcasting White Paper 80
Brown, Gordon 6, 19, 51, 52
Bruner, J. ('Man: A Course of Study') 83, 85, 87
Bryson, Bill 49

Campaign for Labour Party Democracy 19
Canavan, Denis 42
Carter, Jimmy 58
central government 132–40
charities *see* voluntary bodies
charity law 120
Charter 88 5, 36, 154
China 74
Citizen Audit 8, 142–8
Citizen Connect 79–80
citizenship education 53, 81, 85–7
citizen participation 22, 51, 55, 134
Citizenship Foundation 77, 142
citizenship promotion 151–4
citizenship values 48–9, 51, 72–3, 112–13, 139
city culture 66
Civic Forum 121
civic voluntarism 144–5, 146–7
civil society 41, 66–7, 104
Clarke, Martin 44
clause IV 19
Coffield, Frank 94
Cole, G.D.H. 152
Colley, Linda 49, 51, 57
Commission for Citizenship (1990) 100
Commission of Racial Equality 50–1
Common Purpose 142
Communist Party 74
community activists 5, 9
community arts 64, 66, 67, 68, 69–70, 72
community groups 6–7, 123–4
community involvement 60
Community Music London 70
concepts 95–6
Conservative Party 14, 20–1, 24, 117, 132
Constant, Benjamin 1
Constitution Unit 38
Consultative Steering Group (CSG) 37
continuing education 53, 81, 85–7, 90–1
Co-operative Party 75
Copus, Colin 23